POPPY'S

 PUPPIES

Text copyright © 2010 Dogs Trust

First published in Great Britain in 2010 by Hodder Children's Books

The right of Sophia Fergus to be identified as the Author of the Work has been
asserted by her in accordance with the Copyright, Designs and Patents Act 1988.

1

A Catalogue record for this book is available from the British Library

ISBN 978 1 444 90141 2

Book design by Janette Revill

Printed and bound in Great Britain by
CPI Bookmarque Ltd, Croydon, Surrey

The paper and board used in this paperback by Hodder Children's Books
are natural recyclable products made from wood grown in
sustainable forests. The manufacturing processes conform to the
environmental regulations of the country of origin.

Hodder Children's Books
a division of Hachette Children's Books
338 Euston Road, London NW1 3BH
An Hachette UK company
www.hachette.co.uk

POPPY'S

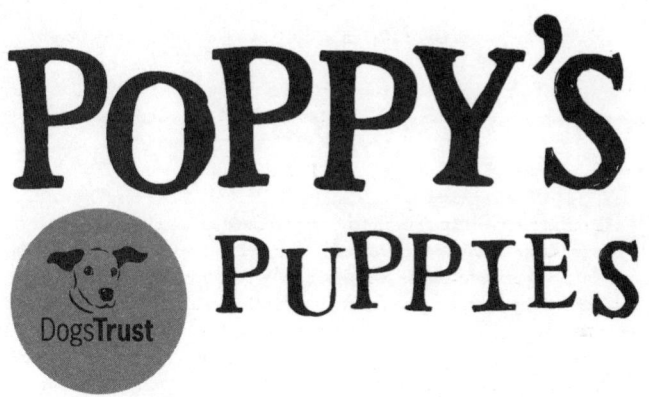

PUPPIES

SOPHIA FERGUS

A division of Hachette Children's Books

To Grace and Ivan

Contents

FOREWORD
BY CLARISSA BALDWIN,
CHIEF EXECUTIVE OF DOGS TRUST

Hello,

I'm Clarissa and I'm proud to be head of the UK's largest dog welfare charity, Dogs Trust. My favourite thing about this wonderful job is knowing that every day we make life better for thousands of homeless hounds by helping them towards safe, happy and healthy futures. In fact, about sixteen thousand dogs' lives are turned around every year thanks to our amazing supporters and the devoted staff at our seventeen rehoming centres across the country.

But if that's the best thing about working for Dogs Trust, the second best is definitely all the dogs I get to meet. I've shaken paws with every sort of pooch you can imagine – massive and miniature, bouncy and doddery, playful and thoughtful, healthy and poorly, speedy and slow, extroverted and introverted, one-eyed, three-legged, woolly, wiry, silky, and even furless.

As unique as every dog is, however, one thing they have in common is that they all started life as a tiny newborn pup. And as every dog-lover knows, those innocent eyes, frantically wagging tails and wiggling bodies, and sheer love for just being alive make puppies one of the greatest joys on this planet.

So this is a book all about puppies.

You'll meet some of the greatest puppy characters to come through Dogs Trust's doors, and you'll get lots of information on how to love and look after your own pup. But most of all, you'll understand how central puppies are to our charity's work. Because just as all dogs grew from pups, all pups will grow into adult dogs, and too often irresponsible puppy purchasers don't think about that.

We are delighted you are reading this book. Your support is so important to us as we campaign for a happy puppyhood for every dog, and to spread our message 'a dog is for life, not just for Christmas'.

For more information about Dogs Trust (and puppies!), please have a look at our website at www.dogstrust.org.uk.

Bye for now,
Clarissa

An Introduction from Poppy, the Dogs Trust Dog

Wag, wag. Hi there readers.

Yes it's me, Poppy, back for a second book! If you've read my first, you'll have met some wonderfully inspiring canines, and you'll know that my job as Dogs Trust Ambassadog keeps me very busy indeed. As well as being a best-selling authoress, my responsibilities include writing a regular column for *Wag!* magazine, responding to emails from fans, making celebrity appearances and posing for various photo shoots. When I'm in the office at Dogs Trust HQ I also make it my daily duty to roll over and allow my belly to be tickled (this makes my colleagues smile and seems to relax them), and to clear everybody's bins of leftover lunch (or any wrapper that smells like it may have previously contained lunch).

And it's while I'm carrying out these snuffling and chewing-based tasks that I do my most serious thinking. It was on Wednesday the twenty-third of December last year that the subject for this book came to me. I was lying in bed at the office, tearing a cheese and pickle-scented napkin into small pieces, when my colleague Liz received the phone call that we all dread at this time of year. She looked so sad when she hung up. I put down my cheesy treat and walked over to let her ruffle my fur as she told everyone in the office how the tiniest Jack Russell you've ever seen had just been found in a park in Leeds. He was abandoned, freezing, and so sick he might not live.

Every year Dogs Trust works hard to spread the message that 'a dog is for life, not just for Christmas', but still every year puppies are abandoned because they are given as presents to people who don't really want them or can't take care of them properly. We are a happy lot here at Dogs Trust, and no one enjoys Christmas more than us. But at the same time as getting excited about the presents and parties and big dinners, we are also awaiting that sad phone call with news that the first 'unwanted gift' of the year has been handed in to us.

When I heard how Tiny Tim had been found and brought to our rehoming centre that day, I knew I had to tell his story. And this made me think about the thousands of other amazing puppies I've known in my job. I've had my ears chewed and my tail pulled by every type of puppy you can imagine, and each with a different tale to tell. But these pups have all had one thing in common. They are so sweet you can't help squealing with delight when you see them. Well humans squeal with delight, I usually squeal when I get a tiny set of teeth clamped around my ankle. But the fact remains – there is something purely perfect about a puppy.

So as well as Tiny Tim, I'm going to introduce you to some more of the cutest pups I've ever met. Each one has had a tricky start in life, but their stories are an inspiration to us all. We have *Blue Peter* celebrity, Barney, and lord of the manor Otto. There's Rhys, whose talents make his owner's life a hundred times easier, and young Snowy, who needs a little extra help to get by. You're about to know what it's like to look after abandoned puppies for a living, you'll understand why puppy farms are terrible places, and you're going to meet a dog who looks like Elvis Presley!

You will also find all the puppy information you need in 'Poppy's Pointers'. We must never forget that for the endless fun and happiness a puppy brings, we have to make many serious promises and a massive commitment in return. A dog is for life, after all. My pointers will help you to determine whether your home could be a happy place for a new baby dog to grow up. And if you're already a proud owner, you'll find lots of information on how to understand and take care of your pup, and how to enjoy a lovely life together.

Introduction

But before all this, readers, I must introduce you to a special friend and colleague of mine. He is new to Dogs Trust HQ, and still has lots to learn, but I am confident that in a few years' time he'll have a better understanding of the work and may even be able to take over some of my duties. He already rolls over happily for a tummy-tickle, and raids waste paper baskets enthusiastically, but his technique is not very good and I would still rather do those jobs myself. What Daniel lacks in skill, however, he makes up for in fun, energy and the biggest, softest ears in the world. I can't wait for you to meet him.

Ladies and gentlemen, it is my pleasure to present my dear friend and eager apprentice, Dogs Trust's very own Daniel the spaniel!

Lots of licks,
Poppy xxx

Daniel the Spaniel

'I didn't want a puppy to start with,' says Deana, smiling at Daniel and Maggie, who are involved in a noisy game of tug between the desks at Dogs Trust HQ. Maggie always wins this game, being the big, solid golden retriever that she is. She stands heavy and still with one end of the toy clamped between her teeth, while Daniel the spaniel grabs the other end and tries to shake it from her grip. He makes all sorts of unearthly growling noises as he waggles his little head and jerks his body, and runs backwards. Gentle Maggie just blinks at him, wagging her big tail and not budging an inch. Eventually Daniel loses his grip and flies backwards, landing on Deana's feet.

'Oof!' she exclaims, patting the glossy auburn-and-white bundle and accepting a little lick. 'In the past I've always been much more of an old dog person. And I like ugly oldies at that, or what some other people might call ugly. I love really elderly staffies and doddery old crossbreeds – dogs that our centres usually struggle to rehome. I'm not usually drawn to classically beautiful dogs like Daniel, but there was just something about him. It only took a couple of meetings before I badly wanted to adopt him, but I had a terrible, nail-biting wait to find out if I could.'

By the time Deana met Daniel for the first time, he had already been through a lot in his short life. His first owners were a lovely couple in the north of England who had dreamed about getting a spaniel for many years. They were kind, responsible people and knew how much time and energy a puppy takes up, so they waited until they retired before they got one. When the day came, and they fell in love with an excitable auburn-and-white speckled pup, they took him home and named him Daniel. Daniel loved his new home and his new family adored him too. Spaniel ownership was even more fun than they had imagined. They shared a few happy weeks getting to know each other. But then, one day, they received some awful news.

One of Daniel's new owners was diagnosed with a very serious illness that might last for a long time. The family knew it wouldn't be fair to keep the puppy when they were worried about other things and couldn't give him the attention he needed. But they consoled themselves with the thought that because their beloved pup was still so young and silky-furred he had a good chance of having a happy life in a different home. So with tears in their eyes, they drove the puppy they had waited so long to own all the way to Dogs Trust Darlington.

Little did young Daniel know, his life was about to take another unusual turn.

A few days before Daniel's arrival, Dogs Trust HQ had called Darlington rehoming centre with a mysterious request, and manager Sue was on the lookout. As the little spaniel trotted innocently through the doors that day, Sue spotted him and wondered, *Could this be the puppy we're looking for?*

She bent down to greet him and was delighted. She knew as well as anyone that puppies could be amazing, but when Sue first saw Daniel, she thought he was wonderful in every way. He was happy, bubbly and enthusiastic, and wriggled his little body with excitement in that way that only spaniels seem to do. He was very friendly and eager to meet the other dogs in reception, but he wasn't out of control. He was young, healthy and beautiful, with soft auburn-and-white dappled fur. At first Sue was baffled as to why such a nice couple would want to give up a puppy like this.

Daniel the Spaniel

But when she heard about the illness, she agreed that perhaps it was the best thing to give Daniel a chance to start again. She took down lots of details about what sort of dog he was, the games he liked to play and the food he liked to eat, and she assured his owners that she would find him the happy new home he deserved.

Once Sue had settled Daniel into a cosy kennel, given him a meal and bowl of water, and made big a fuss of him, she got straight on the phone to Dogs Trust HQ with the news.

'I think our search may be over,' she said. 'If this puppy doesn't have star quality, I don't know who does.'

The mission to find the perfect pup was so top secret that even Sue didn't know all the details. She had been asked to look for a pretty, friendly, outgoing puppy with bags of charm for a mystery job on TV. He or she needed to be bright, easy to train and happy around people and animals. Most importantly, the puppy had to be calm and unfazed by lots of activity going on, because TV studios can be hectic places.

So she took some photos of Daniel and emailed them to HQ, where everyone gathered around the computer to look. A chorus of squeals went up as they admired the soft, curly fur on his ears, his sweet, expressive eyes and the brown splodges on his pink belly.

Those at HQ in charge of the secret mission nodded to each other, agreeing that in just two months this innocent pup could be one of the most famous dogs in the country. He had the potential to take on one of the most important and long-standing positions at the BBC.

Daniel could be the new *Blue Peter* dog.

Photos and descriptions of puppies poured in from all of Dogs Trust's seventeen rehoming centres in response to the mysterious challenge, but Daniel shot to the top of the list. And there he remained until news came in one morning about another possibility – an adorable dachshund/red setter cross called Barney. Calm, confident and upbeat, the unusual auburn crossbreed also had all the qualities required of a TV star and BBC executive.

The *Blue Peter* presenter who would be the lucky puppy's owner called to say she was very excited about having a new family member and canine colleague. She would be coming to Dogs Trust Harefield in two months to choose the pup, who would have to be ready to start work straight away.

There was no time to lose. Barney and Daniel had wonderful potential to be celebrity dogs, but they were by no means ready to work in a TV studio where they would be watched by millions of people. Neither of them had been tested in such unusual surroundings before. What if Daniel chewed through the camera leads? What if Barney peed on the set?

To be prepared for their 'job interviews' the pups needed training, socialisation and to get used to lots of different situations. And because of the strange circumstances, it was agreed that they would be fostered, or temporarily rehomed, by two members of Dogs Trust staff. Richard, manager of the rehoming centre at Harefield, fostered Barney, while David, who was an assistant field director, travelled to Darlington to collect Daniel.

'I had never fostered a dog before but I have to admit I was really looking forward to having a puppy around,' says David. 'My wife Helen and I own three dogs and two cats already, so we thought ours would be a great foster home for Daniel. All the dogs sleep in our bedroom, so we squeezed all the beds together and managed to fit Daniel's little bed alongside them. It was very cute, a bit like living with a baby!'

Daniel settled into life at David and Helen's quickly. He was warmly welcomed by the other three dogs, and quickly started learning how to get on with different sorts of characters.

'Just being at home was great training for him,' says David. 'We've got Nobby who's four – a great but grumpy wheaten terrier. Lucy is a big, bouncy, loving labrador. She's always full of beans and wanting to play. And three-legged lurcher Megan is like the old lady of the house, very grown-up and not into these puppy games at all. They all loved Daniel, and in their different ways, each one taught him how to be a dog.'

Daniel and Lucy became firm friends and playmates straight away. Lucy was overjoyed to have a friend who wanted to play with her, and Daniel was full of love and admiration for the two-year-old lab. He followed her around everywhere.

The pup also received a good education in cats. He learned from Sabina that cats can sometimes be great friends. 'Sabina thinks she's a dog anyway,' says David. 'She and Lucy often play together.' But it was perhaps the older tom cat, Spud, who taught Daniel a more important lesson about how to behave around cats. 'Spud disciplines dogs,' says David. 'Usually, if a puppy is introduced to a cat, the first instinct is to try and play. But it's important for puppies to learn that not all cats will be happy about this, and they can't go through life chasing every cat they see. Whenever Daniel got too playful or boisterous with Spud, the cat would turn around and whack him across the nose with his paw. So Daniel quickly learned to treat cats with some caution, and developed a healthy respect.'

Another challenge that Daniel faced was how to use stairs. We sometimes forget that even basic things we do without thinking can be a big challenge for someone who has only been in the world for a few months. And it took this little spaniel a long, long time to get used to stairs. 'He also learned to go up before he could come down,' David says. 'So if he followed the other dogs upstairs he couldn't then follow them down again. Sometimes I would notice he was missing and I'd go to the stairs and there was his little face peering down from the top.'

The first time the puppy came into work at Dogs Trust HQ, he was still very uncomfortable with stairs, but David worked on the first floor, so he got lots of practice. 'Coming to work with me was an important part of his *Blue Peter* training,' says David.

When he trotted in on his first day, everyone stood up from their desks to see the new furry face and potential superstar. A little crowd gathered around him. Office dogs Poppy, Reuben and Maggie all came over to say hello and give him a sniff and a wag. He met Barney too, his competitor for the TV job, though you wouldn't know the two were rivals. Daniel was such a friendly, laid-back little chap that everybody was charmed.

But it was Deana, editor of *Wag!* magazine, who fell for him the hardest. 'I'd been considering getting a dog for a while,' she says. 'But I was thinking about a grown-up dog. I got my last dog Angel when she was very old, and she was wonderful. Whoever I chose this time would have to be just like her in lots of ways. He or she would have to be a dog who was happy to commute to work on the bus, someone who got on well with everyone in the office, and most importantly, someone who would be good with children.'

Deana's two daughters, Rachel and Sara, knew their mum was on the lookout for a family dog because they had all discussed it lots of times and agreed they were ready for the commitment. They decided that after they got back from a holiday to America, they would start their search. No one expected Deana to fall in love with a dog so soon, or that she would so desperately want a dog like Daniel. 'He was so *pretty*,' she says. 'And you know that's not my style at all! Where were the creaky legs? Where was the patchy greying fur? But he was so sweet, and the two of us just clicked. He kept bringing toys up to my desk and asking me to play with him. How could I resist?'

Over the following few weeks, Daniel became more and more confident and happy. He grew bigger and now flew up and down the stairs without a care in the world. He was fully toilet-trained, as almost from the beginning he copied David's other dogs and always went in the garden. David and Helen took him out and about as much as they could to get him used to meeting lots of different people and animals. As well as going to Dogs Trust, he sometimes went to work with Helen, who was a veterinary nurse. And on the weekends, they all went together to lots of bustling country fairs. Before long, Daniel was completely at ease with friends, strangers, adults, children, dogs, cats, horses, cows, sheep and any other animal you could think of.

He was looking more and more like a *Blue Peter* dog every day. But every day Deana found herself wishing he wasn't. She realised that she was dreaming *she* could be Daniel's new owner. She told her husband Alex about him, who thought he sounded lovely too, and a great dog for the two girls. They eventually agreed that if Daniel wasn't picked for *Blue Peter*, they would take over from David and Helen as his owners. They decided not to tell their daughters, Rachel and Sara, because the disappointment if he was chosen would be too much to bear.

Once Deana and Alex had made their decision, Deana spoke to David, who welcomed the news. 'I'm not as much of a softie as my wife,' he says. 'In my job I see so many homeless dogs, all of them gorgeous and all equally deserving of new homes. We were only ever fostering Daniel, we were never going to be his permanent owners. But if it was just up to Helen, our house would be stuffed full of dogs – she would take in every one she sees if she could! And she did get very attached to Daniel.'

As the time for *Blue Peter*'s decision drew closer, Deana and Alex became more and more nervous.

The family's two-and-a-half week holiday to America was approaching and Deana really hoped she would find out before then, but as the day of the flight arrived she had come to terms with the fact that she wouldn't. She adored Daniel so much by this point that she didn't want to think about what would happen if they couldn't have him.

The family checked-in at the airport and were getting ready to board the plane. As Deana and the two girls went to the toilet, Deana's phone rang in her bag. She scrabbled to answer it. From the huge grin that spread across Deana's face, Rachel and Sara knew something big was happening. 'And that's when I told the girls that in two and a half weeks we would be getting a puppy. The noise that came from the two girls was astounding! It was a great moment. There was so much shouting and jumping around in that toilet at Heathrow. And for the whole time we were in America, they talked about nothing else. They couldn't wait to get home to their new puppy.'

David and Helen were more than happy to look after Daniel the spaniel for a bit longer while Deana and family were on holiday. 'I was actually almost certain *Blue Peter* would choose Daniel,' says David. 'But now, I can see that they made the right decision. Barney's completely at home on that TV set. It's lovely for Daniel that he gets to be part of such a happy family, and it's lovely for me that I still get to see him at work all the time.'

So Daniel became Deana's dog. Helen was upset to see him leave, but knew he had to. She packed up his bed, his toys and his favourite chews, and she wrote Deana a letter expressing how happy she was that he was going to a lovely home. She shared everything she had learned about Daniel whilst he lived with her – his favourite games, his little habits, everything she could think of. And Deana went to pick him up.

That first evening Daniel came home with her, he got an upset stomach. 'It's very common when a pup goes into a new home environment,' says

Deana. 'It's a confusing time, and can often end in a few yukky accidents! He was so lovely though, after we sorted him out and gave him a bath, he hopped straight on to the sofa, put his head in my lap and went to sleep.'

And then very quickly, Daniel grew to love his new home. 'He adores the girls,' says Deana, 'and they love him too.' Sara, who's four, likes to stroke the wavy white stripe that runs down the pooch's auburn back. 'It's S for spaniel,' she says.

'He's a wonderful office dog, but I suppose he

could work a bit harder,' says Deana. 'When he's not rolling around on the floor or playing with Maggie, he spends a lot of time looking for things to chew. He likes cardboard, but best of all he likes to eat shoes. He destroyed a pair of our workmate Sally's best shoes recently and I had to buy her a new pair.'

But no one would change Daniel for the world. He has a huge gift for relieving stress. If anyone is having a hard day at work, spending some time with Daniel is the best medicine they can get. And Deana is the luckiest of everyone, because she gets to spend all day every day with him. 'He comes with me everywhere,' she says proudly. 'He's like my speckled shadow. He may not be the *Blue Peter* dog, but in our house he's treated like a star anyway. And if you see the way he sits sometimes, perched on the back of the sofa looking all regal and important, you can see he feels like one too.'

It is a myth that dogs are colour-blind – they can see in colour, just not as vividly as humans.

An average dog can run up to nineteen miles per hour when running at full speed, but the members of the greyhound family are the fastest. They can run up to forty-five miles per hour.

The common dog name Fido comes from the Latin word for *faithful* or *fidelity*.

The fur of a newfoundland is highly water resistant and, because of their webbed paws, they are also excellent swimmers. Bassett hounds, on the other hand, can hardly swim.

A dog's temperature is between 38 and 39.2 degrees Celsius.

Barney on the Box

Sniff, sniff, lick! Hello, Poppy here.

While I was at the office yesterday I came across an old newspaper under a colleague's desk. I was trying to decide whether to shred it into tiny pieces, which is always quite satisfying, or possibly just lie on it and go to sleep. Then, on the front page of the paper, I recognised a photograph of a favourite dog friend of mine, Barney the *Blue Peter* dog.

I sometimes think humans don't always understand how brilliant we dogs are. And we're often too modest when it comes to our many talents as well. But Barney's story is a good example of a deserving dog reaching the dizzying heights of stardom. Just another abandoned pup, Barney went from nowhere to being one of the most famous doggy faces in the country.

People often ask me what it's like to be a celebrity dog. How do I cope with the pressures of fame? I simply tell them my three golden rules: ears up, tail tall and don't let anything ruffle your fur. Of course, by now I'm used to all the excitement I cause whenever I make an appearance. I feel a duty to my public because I realise what a thrill it is for people to shake my paw or ruffle my ears. I especially enjoy meeting children. I always try to look my most adorable for kids and, what can I say? They love me!

But that's enough about me. Don't you hate it when dogs talk about themselves all the time? I'm so glad I'm not like that. Anyway, the story you're about to read is a truly uplifting one – a tale of adventure, fame and excitement. Oh, and chicken! I hope you like it.

Lick, lick,

Poppy xxx

Barney and his brother Beanie were scampering, owner-less and collar-less along the side of a road, when a kind passer-by found the two lost pups and took them to a local rescue centre. Days passed but nobody came to collect the puppy brothers, and as the centre became full, the manager started investigating other rescue charities that could help. Soon, Barney and Beanie were on their way to Dogs Trust Harefield.

Richard, who is the manager at Harefield, went to the puppy block to meet the pair of pups. He especially remembers the moment he saw Barney for the first time. 'Both of them were adorable but Barney really was a special little chap,' he says. 'He had a really cute face and a long, flowing, reddish-tan coat. He looked like a stretched out, slightly-too-big dachshund.'

There was a reason Richard was taking a particular interest in puppies that day. Just before Barney and Beanie arrived, Dogs Trust had received an exciting secret request. They were to look out for a puppy who could have the potential to follow in the pawsteps of the well-known woofers Petra, Patch, Shep, Goldie, Bonnie, Meg, Mabel and Lucy to become the ninth *Blue Peter* dog. The lucky pup would be adopted by one of the presenters of the show, Helen, and would be on TV regularly in front of millions of viewers.

Quite a destiny for an abandoned pup!

So when Richard met Barney, he immediately thought about this secret mission. And as they got to know each other, he became increasingly sure that Barney had what it took. 'While Beanie was excitable and a bit naughty, more interested in causing mischief than anything else, Barney just wanted to be everybody's friend and to make them happy,' says Richard. 'He really just wanted to be a good boy, and we realised quickly that would make him easy to train.

'So with his sweet personality and his eager, responsive behaviour I was sure he would fit the part,' Richard continues, 'but I didn't know how he would cope with all the different situations he would come across in such a demanding job. I wondered how he would behave in different sorts of environments, how he would react around children and how he would take to housetraining. These were important questions for a *Blue Peter* dog. How would he respond to all those people and cameras around him? I decided to foster him temporarily to see how he got on with my home and family. My wife works mostly from home, so there is always someone about, and fostering works out really well.'

A few days later, after they had all their health checks at the centre, Beanie was rehomed to a lovely new family with children and another dog to play with, and Barney too went to his first real home. 'That first day he was so excited to be out of the kennels and with a family of his own,' says Richard. 'We have six other dogs and a big black-and-white moggie called Pogo. Barney got on with everybody from the beginning, and Pogo was a special favourite because they were almost the same size! Then Wilma, my huge, affectionate, lady dog weighing almost nine stone, became like his mum. Barney adored snuggling up to her and licking her face.'

The pretty pup was quickly house-trained and settled into family life easily, just as Richard expected. Of course, there were a few mistakes. 'One day I came home to find Barney chewing up my favourite trainers. He was wagging his tail and looking at me like it was the best thing in the world to do. It was then we started to teach him what he should chew rather than what he *shouldn't*. But we gave him lots of encouragement when he got it right, because positive training is always the best way to get through to any dog.'

Barney's great love of cheese made training even easier, because it was his favourite reward. And chicken is his other great love. 'He would eat it every day if he could,' says Richard. 'But he had to learn that puppy food was the best thing for him at his age.'

Barney made a strong bond with Richard's two-year-old son Jack, and liked nothing more than to sit on the little boy's knee and give him lots of licks. 'They were partners in crime,' laughs Richard. 'I would watch them pottering off down the garden together and wonder what sort of mischief they were planning to get into this time.'

The more Richard got to know Barney, the more convinced he was that the pup was right for *Blue Peter*. But he still had to see if he would be able to deal with different, strange situations, and with travelling. 'Of course the first thing we did was to take him to the park, where he met lots of other dogs and people,' Richard says. 'He loved it and was soon chasing around happily. A favourite trick would be to run full speed at a dog, then spin in a circle, do a kind of foot-shuffle and shoot off in a different direction, leaving the puzzled dog wondering where he had gone. It was brilliant fun to watch!'

Richard and his family took Barney on a train journey that went very well indeed. A car trip didn't go so smoothly, and like many puppies, poor Barney was car sick. Next Richard took him to Watford town centre to see how the little dog would deal with crowds, and that was a great success. Barney was displaying star qualities already. He often sat in the rehoming centre reception to watch all the people and dogs coming and going. To Richard's delight, he especially loved meeting children and really seemed to thrive on their attention.

By the time he had been with them for a few weeks, Richard and his family had become really attached to Barney. 'I've fostered a lot of dogs before,' says Richard. 'But I've always been happy for them when they leave for new homes. I've looked after injured wild animals too, knowing from the start that they would have to leave when they were well enough. And I was always happy to see them released into the wild. But Barney was such a special little dog, I knew it was going to be hard to say goodbye. I remember how he liked to snuggle up to us as close as he could, or fall asleep on his back with his legs in the air. Sometimes he would sleep upstairs in our bed. He liked to be under the sheets with his head on the pillow. The first thing you woke up to was a wet nose!'

It was approaching the time for Barney and another dog, Daniel, to meet Helen from *Blue Peter*. She was coming to Dogs Trust Harefield and would have to decide between them. Richard almost hoped that she wouldn't choose Barney because he and all his family – including the dogs and cat – were so attached to the little chap. 'But at the same time I was excited about the wonderful life he would have ahead of him if he was chosen,' Richard says.

TV presenter Helen was delighted that everything in her life was finally in place for her to own a dog. 'I grew up with dogs and really missed having one in my life,' she says. 'My family lived on a farm and we always had sheepdogs and labradors. There's always been someone in the family with a dog. But because I go to work and live alone, for ages it wasn't possible to have one,' she explains.

Then one day the *Blue Peter* managers suggested that Helen should adopt a dog who could become another member of the *Blue Peter* team. 'They told me that they would help to look after a dog if I got one,' she says. 'I do a lot of travelling in my job, but they said that whenever possible he could come with me. And of course we would be working together so he wouldn't be on his own at home all day.

'I was really happy about the idea, especially because we would be giving a home to an abandoned dog. I spent a lot of time with Dogs Trust, and they analysed me thoroughly to see what kind of dog would be best, to make sure that we'd be happy together. I think that's so important.'

The day finally came and Helen arrived at Dogs Trust Harefield to choose between the two carefully selected puppies. Richard took them to the special puppy play area where Helen was waiting. Daniel, the little auburn-and-white spaniel, started bouncing around excitedly straight away, wanting to play with Helen, whereas Barney just wanted to roll over and have his tummy tickled.

'It was amazing meeting the puppies – but awful too!' Helen says. 'I didn't want to say no to either of them. They were both beautiful, but

Barney seemed a bit more affectionate and I really liked how he just wanted to be close to me.'

Helen knew Richard's family had looked after Barney for a long time and didn't like to take him away from them, but after an agonising decision, it was finally settled. Because of his lovely nature, beautiful dark eyes, and long, silky, red fur, Helen decided that it had to be Barney.

'He fluttered his eyelids at Helen a few too many times for her to resist!' laughs Richard. 'And I think that won the day! Of course it was a sad day when he left. But so exciting as well. There were a lot of photographers there at the time, and I think all the attention and the limelight distracted him. I remember he gave Helen a huge kiss.'

'When I took Barney away, the poor thing was nervous at first,' says Helen. 'He hated the car and was violently travel sick.' Barney went back to Helen's home on Friday night a worried puppy, but by Monday morning his confidence had sprung back and he was like a different dog.

On his first day at work in the *Blue Peter* studio, he didn't seem at all nervous about his strange new surroundings, and just wanted to play with the other animals. There was Lucy, a beautiful twelve-year-old golden retriever and Mabel, a border collie with one blue and one brown eye who had been on the show for an astonishing fourteen years. There were also two cats called Socks and Cookie, and, of course, Shelley the tortoise. 'It was hilarious,' says Helen. 'The others had all been there for years and compared to him they seemed so sensible and street-wise. Barney was like a kid who wanted to play all the time. Sometimes they'd look at him and seem to raise an eyebrow, as if to say, "All right, pipe down now." He was the chirpy toddler who liked to wind them up. He licked the cats all the time, which they really didn't like as you can imagine!'

Helen has a hectic life working with *Blue Peter* and travels much of the time. Earlier this year, she

42

completed a two-thousand-mile trip kayaking up the River Amazon for charity, and set a world record. But when Helen's *Blue Peter* trips take her closer to home, Barney loves being her travel companion and often stays with her in hotels. 'He likes it when people recognise him as the *Blue Peter* dog. He's a real attention seeker,' laughs Helen. 'He loves company and he'll even howl if nobody takes any notice of him!'

At home though, Barney likes to do normal doggy things. Nothing is better than sitting on Helen's knee or lying at her feet. Sometimes he will tear around, squeaking his squeaky ball. Chicken is still his favourite food and he still can't get enough of it. He sometimes stays on the family farm where he has a perfect holiday with Helen's mum.

He loves going for long walks and chasing birds, and he is starting to understand what on earth Helen is doing when she throws a ball in front of him!

Barney is now about two years old, although no one knows his exact age. His life is unrecognisable from when he and his brother were just two strays wandering by the side of the road. From being a lost puppy, he found his way to Dogs Trust, and then to a loving foster home with Richard's family. And now he has become a national television personality with a devoted owner for life. But despite everything, Barney's still the same happy little dog who adores chicken and a joyous run in the park.

'When we watch Barney and Helen on TV it's lovely to see how great they are together,' says Richard. 'Barney loves everybody, and nothing could ever change that. We've had lots of celebrities here at Dogs Trust Harefield, from Hollywood actors to pop singers to TV personalities, but without a doubt Barney will always be my favourite.'

People in ancient China stayed warm by carrying toy dog breeds in their sleeves.

Like people, dogs find comfort and happiness in touching another living being, which is one reason why man and dog get along so well. Studies show that a lovingly handled dog is healthier, happier and better behaved.

The earliest dog fossil dates back to nearly 10,000 B.C.

Dalmatian puppies do not have any spots on them when they are born. The spots actually develop as they get older.

Poodles were originally bred to be water dogs. Their funny haircuts were meant to keep their vital organs and joints warm while in the water, but now they are just for show.

Saving Otis

Lick, lick. Hi readers.

So your family is having the big important meeting to decide whether to bring a new dog into the household. The word 'puppy' has come up many times over the past few weeks, but this is Decision Day. You are all sitting around the table, or maybe in the living room, having a long discussion about who would feed, walk and play with this new furry family member. What breed of dog should he be? You've talked about where he could sleep, whether your garden is big enough, how much money it would cost to look after him, and how much time you have to spend with him.

With furrowed brows, you look at each other, nodding earnestly. You all agree. Your home is right for this. Your family is ready. The time is right for everyone to make the massive canine commitment that will last for many years to come. You are getting a puppy.

You are getting a puppy!

Suddenly the news sinks in. You leap from your chairs and dance around the room uncontrollably. You hug, whoop with excitement, and all talk at once. The serious faces are gone and it's huge grins and laughter all round. Moments this exciting don't happen every day.

Now the big decision has been made, all that's left to do is think about the fun things, right? Things like choosing a name, a collar and tag, a bed and toys? Well sorry readers, but I'm afraid there is one more very serious decision to make. And it's one that could affect your pup's health, your life together and ultimately the lives of many other puppies.

You must decide *where* you will get your puppy from.

It is true that most breeders are kind, dog-loving

folk who adore their pups and do everything they can to ensure they are healthy and happy, and that they go to proper new homes. But sadly, not every dog is bred by people who care, or given this kind of positive start in life. And even more sadly, many people who buy a new puppy have no idea that they are giving their money to people who treat dogs very badly indeed.

Meet Otis. His story shows once and for all that there are good places and bad places to get a puppy from. You can help pups like Otis too by reading my pointer on 'Choosing your pup' at the back of this book. Once you know what to look out for, you won't have to worry that you are accidentally supporting bad breeding.

I think of little Otis every time I hear that someone's bought a puppy from a suspicious source, and now I hope you will too.

Lots of love,
Poppy xxx

'At Dogs Trust we're always telling people to be aware of where their puppy has come from,' says Sinead, who works at the charity's HQ in London. 'Unfortunately some people breed dogs without a single concern for doggy health and welfare. They view the pups as a "product" and only care about the money they make from selling them. This can mean the puppies and their mothers are kept in very bad conditions, which the innocent puppy-buyer never sees.

'As a charity that campaigns for the wellbeing of dogs and speaks out about bad breeding practices, we decided that we must see for ourselves what it's like to buy a puppy from an unscrupulous dealer, or a "puppy farm" as they're called. Sian, who's a vet nurse from our Harefield rehoming centre, and I decided we should investigate.'

As they were experts on all things canine, they knew the suspicious signs to look out for. 'When you're buying a puppy, you should beware of places that sell more than one breed, and definitely avoid those offering more than three,' Sinead says. 'We did some online research and found a place that was selling four different breeds. We called and made an appointment.'

So the next day, the two dog-lovers set off in the car with a map, feeling anxious but determined to undertake this project. 'I was prepared to be upset by what we found,' says Sinead. 'But because I had read so much about what goes on in puppy farms, and seen so many websites about them, I wanted to see first-hand what really goes on out there.'

They followed the map and eventually found

the address. 'The nerves really began to kick in when we turned the car into the driveway,' Sinead says. 'It was a large house, with a separate building attached to the side, like a big wooden stable block.

'There was a transport van in the driveway – the kind used to move litters from the big puppy farms in the country where the actual breeding happens, to these sites where people come to buy the pups. The conditions were likely to be much worse on the actual farm where the breeding bitches were kept, than this "respectable" front.'

If the people in charge knew the girls were from Dogs Trust, they would certainly not be welcome, so as they went into the house, Sinead and Sian played dumb. 'When we met the man who would be showing us the pups, we pretended to be silly young girls who knew nothing about dogs,' Sian says. 'We decided the puppy would be for me. I said I'd never been a dog owner before and I wanted a cute fluffy one that I could put in my handbag (something a true dog-lover would never say!). Playing my role became easier as my nerves started to calm down. I said I wanted one that would be quiet and not pee on my nice cream carpet, and asked what he had for me.'

Knowing nothing about who these girls really were, the man showed them into the big block attached to the house. 'The place had been converted into kennels,' Sian says. 'There were several plastic containers for the puppies, and as soon as we saw them we knew these were not the right conditions for tiny pups to be kept in.

'Although the thin layer of sawdust in the containers was clean, dogs need company, things to do, and exposure to humans and normal surroundings to be physically and mentally healthy. These pups were kept in their containers day and night. They had some space to move around but no human contact whatsoever. They had no toys, nothing to chew and nothing to do. The stable block was almost completely dark, and there was only light when people were shown in to look at them. So they were clearly scared of humans because they hadn't been socialised at all. Some of the litters were fighting with each other because they were so frustrated and had nothing else to occupy them.'

There were several litters of puppies in the block – west highland terriers, cavalier spaniels, Jack Russells and border terriers. 'The border terriers were the most distressed,' says Sian. 'The prison-like conditions had affected them badly and they were all gazing up at us, terrified and quivering when we looked into their container.

'There was one little creature in particular that looked so sad and lifeless, with a terribly runny nose. Sinead and I looked at each other and just knew he was the one we had to buy.' Sian pointed at the tiny brown bundle who had pressed himself into the very far corner of his enclosure, and told the man she wanted to have a look at that one. The man frowned and hesitated before bending

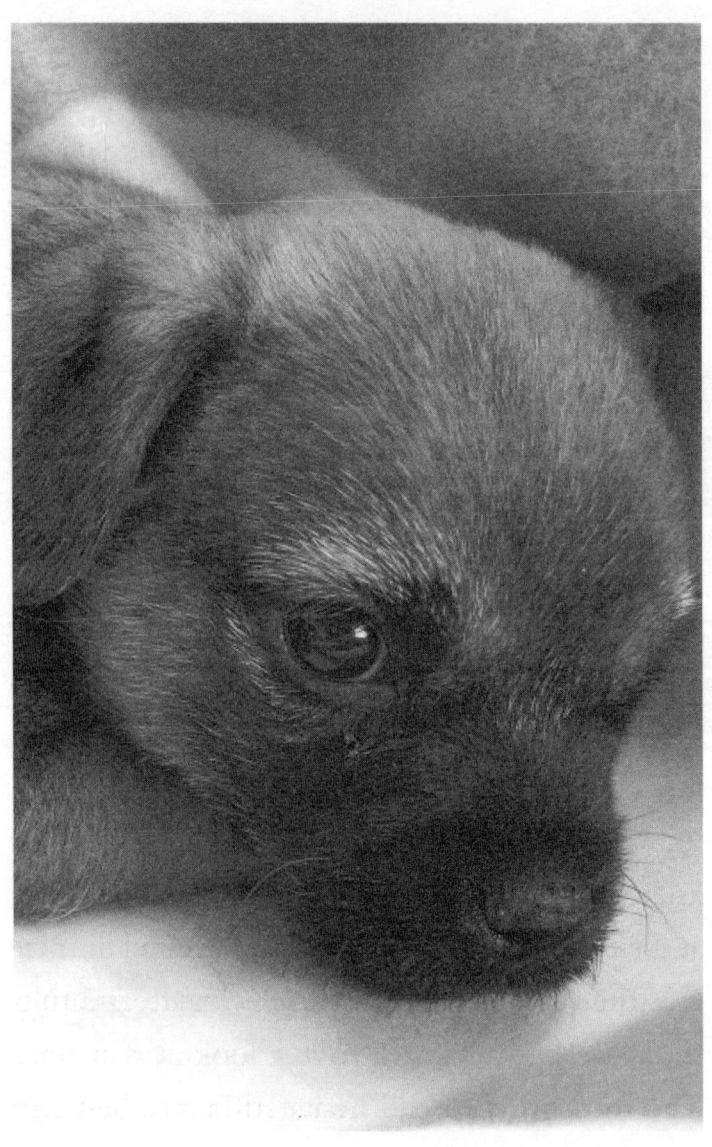

over the side to lift out the quivering little puppy. 'He really didn't want us to choose that one,' Sinead says. 'He knew there was something wrong with him. These rogue breeders don't want to do anything that could expose them, including selling puppies who have been badly affected by their sad existence. Many customers would be deeply upset and furious if they got suspicious, followed the chain back, and saw all the terrible things that go on in the world of puppy farming. In fact Dogs Trust did a study and found that even though ninety five per cent of dog owners said they would never dream of getting a pup from a puppy farm, it's likely that fifteen per cent actually *have*, but without knowing it.

'Perhaps the worst thing about puppy-farming is that the mother of this litter of border terrier pups was almost certainly in a much worse enclosure, with no mental or physical stimulation, and no contact with other dogs or people. Breeding bitches usually have no natural daylight and they are made to have litter after litter until they're too old and then they're replaced by another dog. I can't think about it without getting upset.'

'I said I liked the particularly sad-looking pup because he looked like he was calm and wouldn't be any trouble or bark too much,' says Sian. 'But I was feeling awful inside. Puppies shouldn't be calm. They *should* be trouble, in the most glorious way! They should be eager and full of joy and unable to contain their excitement for just being alive.'

The man tried to tell the girls they couldn't buy the sad little puppy, and asked why they couldn't take another one instead. He tried lots of different tactics, and finally said that the pup the girls had settled on had been reserved by another buyer. But though Sinead and Sian were desperate to save every puppy for sale there, they insisted that the quiet, poorly one was the only pup they wanted. 'In the end we had to leave,' Sian says. 'I said I would come back the next day in case the people who had reserved him didn't turn up.'

So Sian and Sinead went home puppyless, feeling miserable about the lives of the poor pups they had seen, and talking about how awful and unfair puppy farming is.

The next day they returned. The man finally agreed that Sian could have the poor little pup, who was still terribly listless and quiet. 'We were happy I could take the puppy but shocked that the man asked hardly anything about my life and my home,' says Sian. 'He would have sold the puppy to anybody who had the money to pay. Any responsible breeder or rescue charity will ask you lots of questions before they give you a dog. For example, Dogs Trust will not rehome to somebody who works full time, leaving their dog alone in the house all day. We would want to know if there are children and animals in the house, and ask questions that would tell us whether the person was committed, responsible, and knew the serious long-term duties involved in dog ownership. This man couldn't have cared less, as long as I could give him the three hundred and fifty pounds he was asking for. We shuddered to think of the homes that the little lad's littermates might be going to.'

On the eight-hour journey back in the car, the tiny soft ball of fur sat curled up on Sian's lap. 'He was absolutely terrified and totally lifeless. He just lay there dead still but he had a little cough that shook him now and again. It was heartbreaking. We were talking about what we should call him when an Otis Redding song came on the radio. Otis seemed like a lovely name.'

When the girls got back to Dogs Trust, they took Otis to see the vet, who was shocked at the state of the little dog. 'He was very poorly,' says Sian. 'He was underweight with a little pot belly, which meant he was malnourished, and he had a respiratory infection, which was why he was coughing. Otis clearly needed attention that he had not been getting.

'We lifted him off the vet's table and put him on the floor to see how he behaved. A normal, healthy puppy should bounce about energetically, eager for attention and wanting to play. Otis just froze. Then he ran away trembling and pressed himself into a corner of the room, clearly trying to hide. He had no experience whatsoever of the world outside of his litter and his dark, cell-like enclosure.'

The vet was also suspicious about the pup's age. Puppies should stay with their mothers until they are at least eight weeks old, and the man who sold him claimed Otis was indeed eight weeks. But the vet thought he was no more than five or six weeks. 'It's so important that puppies spend enough time with their mothers,' Sian says. 'No person can teach a puppy right from wrong, or about life and the business of being a dog as well as its mum can. We simply speak a different language to dogs, no matter how hard we try to interpret it. So those weeks with its mum are absolutely crucial to every dog's development.'

That night, after the vet had prescribed some antibiotics, Otis went home with Sian. 'I felt so terrible for the helpless little chap who'd had such an awful start in life,' she says. 'Of course we do everything we can at Dogs Trust to make sure our kennels are happy places, but I wanted Otis to start experiencing normal life as quickly as possible.'

It took a good while for the little border terrier to adapt to the world around him. Any kind of noise would frighten him, and he would flinch in terror if anybody approached him or picked him up. But he was good with Sian's other dogs. 'In fact he seemed to find a lot of comfort in other animals. I suppose it's because dogs were all he'd known in that horrible enclosure.' she says. 'He copied what my dogs did and how they approached the world. And slowly he also built up a really good relationship with my mum, who spent all day with him when I was at work. He would follow her around and eventually he'd actually want to be picked up. He'd put his little paws on her knee and ask for cuddles.'

After a few weeks, little Otis had really started to come out of his shell. He'd grown bigger and stronger, his cough had gone, and he'd actually started taking pleasure in the world, having fun and behaving more like a normal puppy. 'It's tragic but it's probably because he was so young that he made quite a good emotional recovery from his ordeal,' Sian says. 'We got him out of that nasty situation quickly and lavished him with kindness and all the things he'd been missing out on in his first weeks of life.

'I wish we could have rescued all his littermates too, but that would have been the wrong thing to do. We always tell people never to buy puppies from breeders like Otis's. Because even though you may be rescuing some puppies, the money you give contributes to creating more puppies and even more suffering in the future. If nobody bought from these people, they could not operate their horrid businesses.'

One day Sian's brother came round to visit with his friend Jamie. 'Jamie is a wonderful dog owner and had been thinking about getting another four-legged friend for a while,' Sian says. 'And when he saw Otis there was instant magic in the air!'

You could tell Jamie had fallen for the little terrier. He knelt down to say hello and Otis wandered over, wagging his tail shyly. 'I purposefully didn't tell Jamie about the pup until he came round that day, but I smiled to myself when they met. I'd suspected they would strike up a lovely friendship, and they did!'

Otis now lives happily with Jamie and a tubby little pug called Lulu, and has the lovely life he deserves. 'He's fully grown now,' says Sian. 'And he's brilliant. A hairy little monkey! Thanks to all the love and care Jamie and Lulu have given him, he's happy around people now and is pretty much like any other normal, well-balanced dog.

'Dogs Trust will keep campaigning to make puppy farming illegal. And in the meantime we're working very hard to tell as many people as possible about what goes on, hopefully stopping potential puppy purchasers from going to these horrid places. We were powerless to do anything to stop and close the place where we got Otis, because the people there were doing nothing illegal. We also know that there are far worse places out there, also operating within the law. So until this type of cruelty is banned it's very important that people are aware of how puppies are sometimes bred, so they are on their guard and know what to look out for.

'You must always ask to see a puppy with its mum, and the conditions that the dogs are kept in should be healthy and suitable. There should be lots of room for the dogs, natural light, water and toys to keep them busy. The breeder should be helpful and open to questions, and they should ask you lots of serious questions in return about whether you can provide a happy home for a dog. The puppies should be bright and alert, and used to human contact. They should be interested in you and run over to you to say hello. And they should look healthy, with clean eyes, ears and bottoms, because bad nutrition or hereditary problems can have lifelong effects on a puppy's health.

'Although we obviously think the best places to get puppies from are charities like Dogs Trust, if people really want a specific breed, we always tell them they can go to breed rescue charities too. Or if you are going to a breeder, make sure you research them thoroughly beforehand and know as much as possible about how they treat their dogs. You should never buy puppies from pet shops, and be very careful indeed about buying from adverts on the internet or in newspapers. Those places that advertise more than one breed are especially suspicious.

© Andrew Aiken

Daniel rescues a drowning stick!

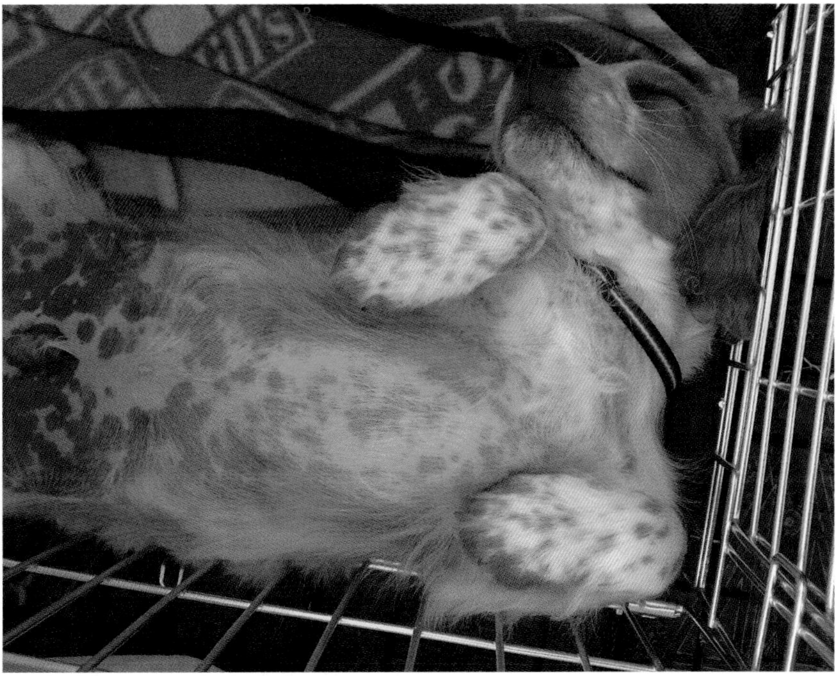

© Pete Rooney

... and hard at work as Poppy's apprentice at Dogs Trust HQ

Daniel the spaniel, in all his speckled glory

Blue Peter's Barney
and Helen pose for
their celebrity shots

Poor little Otis. Who could resist?

'Jamie brought Otis over for a visit just last week. Although it's always so lovely to see his hairy little face and wiry wagging tail, when I look at him I can't help thinking about where he came from and feeling sad. I've told his story so many times, because I think that if everyone knew what Otis and his mother had been through, and everyone followed our simple guidelines, bad breeding like this would no longer exist.'

For advice on where to get a puppy, see page 203.

The breed lundehune has six toes and can close its ears!

A puppy is born blind and deaf.

A puppy is also born without teeth. Aged four to eight weeks, the puppy will develop twenty-eight baby teeth and start to eat solid food. At four to seven months, the baby teeth fall out and are replaced with forty-two permanent adult teeth.

Dogs' nose prints are as unique as humans' fingerprints and can be used to accurately identify them.

Bloodhounds have been used to track criminals for over four hundred years. But even bloodhounds cannot smell the difference between two identical twins.

New Pups on the Block

Woof woof, me again!

As you can imagine, I see lots of children in my job. I've met hundreds of boys and girls of all different ages and from all over the country at our rehoming centres and in my many public appearances as Dogs Trust Ambassadog. Of course, like dogs, every person is different, but one thing I hear again and again from these young dog-lovers is, 'When I grow up, I want to work for Dogs Trust!'

And who could blame them? Imagine spending your days in the company of loads of wonderful woofers, playing with them, looking after them and helping them into happy new lives. And imagine the joy of working in a Dogs Trust puppy block, being surrounded every day with all that puppy love, and even getting paid for it! But, as is the case with lots of jobs, there is much more to being a Dogs Trust Canine Carer than meets the eye.

That's why I thought I would bring you Lisa's story. I'm sorry to say, readers, that Lisa is not actually a puppy. She is a good few years older than the main characters in our other chapters. And what sets her apart even more is that with no tail, two legs and a bald face, Lisa is in fact a *human being*. But as one of the world's most passionate dog-loving human beings in the world, and with one of the most responsible jobs in puppy care in the UK, I hope you will enjoy meeting her nonetheless.

Big wags,
Poppy xxx

'The best two words to describe my average day at work would be crazy and smelly!' says Lisa, grinning from ear to ear. 'I absolutely love my job but it is certainly not for the faint-hearted.'

Lisa has always been a huge dog-lover but twelve years ago she would never have guessed that her career would lead her to the doors of Dogs Trust Merseyside. And she would have been even more surprised to learn that she would one day become the main carer for puppies at the rehoming centre.

'I've been working at Dogs Trust for eleven

years now, and I've been looking after the puppies here for three,' Lisa says. 'Before I came to Dogs Trust I was working in shops, but I had been getting bored with the routine and was thinking about a change of direction in my work. I wanted something that would excite me, where no two days would be the same.'

When she saw the advert in the local paper, Lisa's imagination ran wild. *Doggy Carers wanted for Dogs Trust Merseyside rehoming centre*, the advert said. Lisa had a beautiful fluffy German shepherd at the time and had been spending lots of time training him in agility and taking him to dog shows. 'I've always been really into dogs,' she says. 'I think dog owners are either people who get a dog and then don't think much about them or do much with them, or they are people who want to understand their pet as much as possible and work at developing them. I am that second sort of owner. And I think it was my dedication to dogs that the manager, Georgina, saw when she interviewed me.'

So to her delight, Lisa was offered the job and for eight years she worked happily as a canine carer. 'It was hard, physical work but so rewarding,' she says. As part of the Dogs Trust Merseyside team she fed, exercised and looked after all the homeless dogs that were brought in to the rehoming centre. She loved the fact that every dog's story and every doggy character was different, and took great pleasure in making a real difference to the lives of dogs in need.

Then one day, the lady who was in charge of looking after the puppy block at the centre announced sadly that she was moving to another part of the country and had to leave her job. 'I had always loved filling in on the puppy block,' Lisa says. 'Even though it was such hard work, I found it really interesting and satisfying. There's a lot more to it than just playing with puppies all day.

'What's wonderful about working at Dogs Trust is that canine carers are encouraged to pursue whatever aspect of dogs it is they find interesting.

There are training courses in all sorts of things. For example, some people study all there is to know about dog behaviour and can go on to be Training and Behaviour Advisers. Or some people want to understand more about how to work with difficult dogs. But when the puppy carer left, I told Georgina that I would be really interested in learning more about how to look after puppies and taking over the job on the puppy block.

'Georgina agreed I had what it took to do the job so I was sent on the Puppy Rearing course, which teaches you everything from how puppies are born, to the importance of their relationships with their mother and littermates, to how to socialise pups. It taught me how to wean them from their mother's milk on to solid food, and what sorts of things puppies need to grow up into happy, healthy dogs. It was a really thorough course. I found it fascinating and was really excited about the direction my career was taking.'

Before Lisa could be properly qualified she had

to do a big project. 'I had to do a study of puppies,' she says. 'And then I had to write an essay on all the good and bad things about puppies being in kennels. That made me realise that actually, even though we do lots of wonderful things for pups at Dogs Trust and encourage them to have lots of fun, kennels are simply not the best place for them to grow up. It can be quite stressful and they will always be better off in a loving home environment.

'But we use the time we have with the pups to socialise them, to get them out and about and to make sure they are used to people and other dogs, so when they do go to their permanent homes they will be happy there.'

Lisa was determined to do the best job she could on the puppy block. She decided she would give the residents there the happiest possible start in life, whilst at the same time working hard to find them proper new homes.

But, as excited as she was, Lisa's first day on the

job was still a great shock to the system. 'As soon as I opened the door on that first morning I was greeted with a thousand barks – first for attention and then for food! If you've ever seen the film *Finding Nemo*, the puppies reminded me of the seagull characters – all those little faces shouting at me at once.'

The first job in the morning is to feed the hungry pups. 'Puppies can be very territorial over their food,' Lisa says. 'So there is an art to feeding them, to make sure they don't squabble. If we are giving ten puppies their breakfast, we will put out

at least fifteen bowls of food for them, and dot them around in different places on the floor. This means every puppy will be able to eat in a relaxed way – no one will go hungry and there will be no fights which can lead to behavioural problems later in life. Feeding them this way ensures the puppies will develop calmer characters and be well-behaved around food.

'I put down all the bowls of food outside, and while the pups are busy eating their breakfast, I get down to mopping and scrubbing the kennels clean. I probably do more cleaning than anything else in the puppy block. People don't think about that aspect of being a canine carer, and sometimes it really puts them off when they do. Pups are like babies – they eat a lot and they poo a lot!'

When the rehoming centre has a lot of puppies, their kennels can get quite dirty overnight, so that first clean-up of the day can be a big task. And after that, they are cleaned every hour throughout the day. 'We always put lots of paper down for them, which helps minimise the cleaning,' Lisa says. 'Sometimes though the little monsters decide to be cheeky and bounce around the kennels with their littermates ripping the paper into tiny pieces with their teeth and throwing it about like they're in a snowstorm!

'Even though it's annoying and time-consuming when they do things like that, the silly things the puppies do are one of my favourite parts of my job. My work makes me laugh every day. How many people can say that?'

So, once the kennels are clean, it's a case of

making sure the pups have plenty of blankets and cosy places to sleep, and lots of things to keep them occupied. 'Puppies love to chew,' says Lisa. 'In fact, when their teeth are first coming through, they really need to. So it's important that I put lots of chews in their kennels. I also give them loads of toys. They love all sorts of toys – cuddly ones, squeaky ones, rag pulls. I also give them some cardboard boxes to explore and play in together, which they adore.'

But providing puppies with a good upbringing is not just about socialising them with each other. It is also important that they learn to get along well with humans. 'We are lucky to have lots of volunteers who come and sit with the puppies, and we get staff to play with them as much as possible too, so they get used to being handled by different people,' Lisa says. 'Lots of interaction with people also helps to make up for all the social skills that abandoned puppies miss out on learning from their mothers.

Poppy's Puppies

84

'As well as sitting in the pens with the pups, staff and volunteers also take them out and about around the rehoming centre so they get used to seeing, smelling and hearing adult dogs, lots of activity and different surroundings. We have special little prams that hold a couple of puppies at a time, so if the pups get heavy to carry a volunteer can wheel them around the centre. Sometimes they take them down to the road so the puppies can see what cars look and sound like. There is a train track next to the centre where they also take them to watch the trains going past. Even the fact that the trains cast big shadows is something a puppy can benefit from learning.'

In order to get the little dogs used to the sorts of sounds they will encounter when they eventually go to their new homes, Lisa plays different CDs in the puppy block. 'We have one that has things like fireworks on it, for example. Dogs are often afraid of fireworks, but if they hear the sounds when they are young they will be less likely to be scared of them when they grow up. The CD I play most often though is one called *Everyday Sounds*. It has the sounds of hoovers, TVs, children playing, cats meowing, fire engines, babies crying, and things like that,' Lisa says. 'I'm always trying as hard as I can to prepare the pups for everyday life in an average household.'

One thing the puppy block isn't is an average household. 'Sometimes it gets so hectic,' Lisa says. 'Last year, in just one week, twenty-eight puppies all came in to the centre at once! Can you imagine what hard work it was to feed, exercise, clean and socialise them, not to mention getting them all wormed and vaccinated. They came from four separate litters. There were seven spaniel crosses, five terrier crosses and sixteen other crossbreeds. And though it was strange that they all flooded to the centre at once, an even bigger coincidence was that all apart from one of the puppies was black and white! Local journalists rushed along to see and printed a beautiful photo in the next day's paper.

'There is always a great buzz around the whole rehoming centre when we have lots of puppies,' Lisa says. 'When word gets out, many more families come to visit, because kids are especially excited by puppies. It means everybody has to work harder and help out in the puppy block, because they take so much more feeding, cleaning and general looking after than adult dogs. All the excitement and extra work has a big knock-on effect and totally changes the atmosphere in the whole centre.'

'But then there are times when we have just one or two pups in the puppy block, and if that's the case then I take them home with me overnight. A whole night is a long time for a puppy to be alone, and I just can't bear to shut the door and leave them for all that time. Plus, it means they get a bit of extra socialisation with my shih-tzu Leo and my boyfriend's dog Sidney.'

At the moment there are only two pups in the

puppy block. 'We've got Millie, who's a tiny little thing with a heart murmur, so she needs extra-special looking after,' says Lisa. 'And we've also got Biscuit, who's a Jack Russell/whippet crossbreed and he's beautiful too. Both are booked to go to lovely new homes, so that's great news. It's always much easier to find homes for the puppies than it is for adult dogs, which is often sad for the poor grown-up pooches. In fact puppies are usually only here for a maximum of two weeks.'

Lisa knows she is lucky and that lots of people would love to do her job. 'You need some very important qualities though,' she says. 'You need lots and lots of patience, and you can't mind getting dirty. Walking into a noisy, smelly room first thing in the morning wouldn't be everyone's cup of tea. Of course, you need to have a genuine love of animals, and a real desire to improve their lives.'

But perhaps the most important quality you must have to be a puppy carer is that you mustn't mind hard work. 'I wouldn't change my job for the world,' says Lisa proudly. 'But it's so exhausting! I have to admit, although a roomful of pups is perhaps the most wonderful thing in the world, I always breathe a big sigh of relief when they all leave again to happy new homes!'

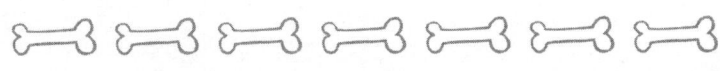

All dogs are descended from wolves, and the two species can still mate. Female wolves have been known to travel great distances to regurgitate full meals for their hungry pups.

The Irish wolfhound is the largest breed of dog but the St Bernard is the heaviest.

Doggy experts believe that every dog on the planet is descended from a species known as the tomarctus – a creature that roamed the earth over fifteen million years ago.

Dogs can be trained to detect epileptic seizures.

Female dogs are only 'in heat', or ready to mate, twice a year for a total of about twenty days. And even then, they will only accept a male for a few of those days.

Snowy Reads the Signs

Hello readers, Poppy here.

You know, if there's one funny thing I've noticed about people, it's how much you lot love to *talk*. Sometimes when I'm at work it really makes me chuckle. All that tittering back and forth, back and forth, all day long. It's endless! I've wondered if maybe it's because you're not very good at expressing yourselves with your bodies. Not having a tail is a big disadvantage. You can't wag your tails so perhaps you wag your tongues instead.

Even though we dogs prefer communicating in more physical ways, it's important we understand a few of our owners' words too. To be honest, I've found ninety-nine per cent of them are pretty pointless, but things like 'walkies' and 'chicken' do actually mean something. It's also useful to know some instructions, like 'sit' and 'come here', so we know what you'd like us to do. And if you want to get our attention just calling our name usually does the trick.

So how do you think a totally deaf puppy gets by in this world of constant talking and listening? I had no idea until I met Snowy. But even though she can't hear a single thing, by just using her sparkly eyes and her brilliant mind, this little dog understands her owner perfectly.

I'm proud to introduce Snowy, the pup who proves that people and dogs were born to talk to each other, and if they can't do it with words, they will always find another way.

Love 'n' licks,
Pops xxx

'Everyone said I was mad,' says Mandy. 'My brother-in-law even asked why I wanted to adopt a deaf dog when there are plenty of dogs with perfect hearing in need of a home. But as soon as he met Snowy, he understood. He admitted he would have snapped her up in a second too if he'd been me. And in fact everyone who doubted my decision soon changed their minds when Snowy charmed their socks off.'

When she first came to Dogs Trust, the pure white pup was tiny. 'I could easily hold her in one hand, and she weighed almost nothing,' says Leslie, who was on reception in the centre that day.

'Even by Jack Russell standards, she was a teeny little thing. And so, so sweet. It's shocking that she ended up abandoned because she was deaf.'

Snowy came into the world by accident. She was born in the home of a breeder, who didn't intend for Snowy's mum to get pregnant. But because she lived with male dogs and the breeder didn't have her spayed, she did. And she gave birth to an adorable but unplanned litter of tiny squirming pups. When they were old enough, the breeder managed to sell all the puppies into new homes, but then, just a week later, one came back.

'It was an awful story,' says Leslie. 'The new owners of this helpless little thing brought her back because they discovered she was deaf. They considered her a defective dog. So they decided they didn't want her, and "took her back" like you would do if you bought a jumper that you then discovered had a button missing. But I don't know how anyone could be so heartless. I've never seen a jumper with such innocent brown eyes and such a lovely temperament as Snowy!'

The breeder's decision to bring the pup to Dogs Trust was kind when you compare it to how some unscrupulous breeders deal with unwanted 'stock', but still, being moved from place to place at only four months old would be difficult for any dog, or any person for that matter.

Snowy's tiny claws made excited scrabbling noises on the reception counter as Leslie popped her up there to take a closer look. Wagging her tail like crazy, and playfully chewing Leslie's fingers, Snowy didn't seem nervous or upset from being shifted around and rejected by two different owners. She was full of energy and had a wonderful zest for life, just like any happy, healthy puppy. She wasn't aware that she had anything physically wrong with her.

'All dogs see the vet when they come in to us,' says Leslie. 'So because we had been told she was deaf, the first thing we wanted to establish was whether or not she could hear at all. The vet only had to do some very basic tests to prove without a doubt that our happy, bouncy little puppy was one hundred per cent deaf. He dropped a ball behind her, and she didn't notice a thing. He clapped his hands and she did not react at all.'

Little Snowy lived in a world of total silence.

'Some people were surprised when we started teaching her sign language,' Leslie says. 'But it's standard practice here. We've had lots of deaf dogs in the past who we've taught to understand sign language. Even my own dogs respond to hand signals as well as voice commands. And actually, it makes sense. Dogs are a lot like humans in the way they understand things. If you imagine a teacher at the front of a classroom, telling everyone to sit down, they will probably make some sort of gesture with their hands too. They give an instruction using sound, but they also emphasise the message visually. Deaf dogs understand in the same way, but because they can't receive the sound, they pay more attention to visual clues.'

And Snowy's passion for people made her the perfect student. 'There was never any problem getting her attention,' Leslie says. 'She adores people so she was always focused on whoever she was with anyway, and always giving her full body wag as if just wagging the tail wasn't enough to express how happy she was to be there.'

Because she was so young, Snowy stayed in the special block at the rehoming centre where all the puppies live. Every day a different canine carer is in charge there. Although looking after a roomful of puppies for a whole day is very hard work, no carer can resist smiling when they find out they are on puppy duty. 'Whoever was working on the block that day would "speak" to Snowy in signs,' Leslie explains.

'The normal way to teach a dog to sit is by holding a treat in front of them, and then by slowly raising it up – the dog's natural response is to sit down,' she continues. 'Of course with a dog who can hear, we say "sit" as well, but with a deaf dog, the raising of the hand becomes the signal to sit. My dogs sit to a hand signal like that too, and they can hear.'

Other signals Snowy learned to understand were 'lie down', which you sign by placing your hand flat and parallel to the ground, and then lower it slowly down. And she quickly learned that 'good girl' was the thumbs-up signal. She would wag her tiny white tail with pride when she got the thumbs-up.

'Snowy was such an exceptional little pup that we thought we must tell the newspapers about her,' says Leslie. 'Everyone loves looking at a picture of a cute puppy, and Snowy was adorable. She was so tiny and unusual-looking with her pure white fur. She had the most amazing attitude to life, and because we'd been teaching her sign language she had a wonderful story too. Lots of journalists came to meet her and take her picture, and the next day she was all over the news. We knew it wouldn't be long before we found her the perfect new home.'

One lady who hadn't spotted Snowy in the papers was Mandy, but she was coming to Dogs Trust that day anyway. 'I'd been thinking for a while that I wanted to get another dog as company for Georgie, my lovely lurcher/collie cross who I'd adopted the year before,' she says. 'And almost as soon as we arrived at the centre I spotted a tiny white puppy in a red jumper playing football on the grass. I couldn't take my eyes off her. It really was love at first sight.'

Mandy had no idea that Snowy was a bit of a celebrity. All she knew was that she desperately wanted to give the playful four-month-old pup a home.

And so after a wonderful meeting with the little dog in the red jumper, full of excitement, licks, wags, cuddles and big grins, Mandy told Leslie she was certain that she could give Snowy the home and life that she deserved. And as she watched Mandy and the pup playing together on the grass outside the centre, Leslie had a strong feeling she was right. Even though the phone was ringing off the hook with people who had seen Snowy in the newspaper and wanted to adopt her, Leslie could see the kind lady and the white puppy with the wildly wagging tail were made for each other.

So Dogs Trust carried out all the proper checks on Mandy's house and lifestyle and decided officially that she could give Snowy everything she needed for a stable, happy home for life. 'I'd never owned a deaf dog before,' Mandy says. 'But I had all the time and patience in the world for this puppy I had fallen so madly in love with. Since the first day I took her home I have never looked back. It was the best thing I ever did.

'Georgie must agree because the two of them are pretty much inseparable,' she continues. 'Georgie loves her to pieces. Snowy came down with an illness quite soon after we got her. She had a very high temperature and needed taking to the vet's straight away. And it was Georgie who told us. The two of them wouldn't usually sleep close together. But that day we found Georgie curled up tight to our pup with her paw over her and looking worried. We knew something was wrong. Thank goodness we got her to the vet's on time, or it could have been very serious.'

The older dog helps to look after the deaf pup in other ways too. 'If we're all out on a walk together, and Snowy runs off out of sight, Georgie will go and bring her back,' says Mandy, proud of her glossy black-and-white crossbreed. 'Snowy obviously can't hear me if I call so I've put three little cat bells on her collar so I have an idea where she is. And because Georgie understands the pup needs a bit of help, she shares the responsibility of rounding her up and bringing her back as well.'

Snowy loves her walks, and is a big fan of big sticks. 'She'll always run off and return with a stick that she then insists on carrying for at least a mile,' Mandy says. 'And it's always huge – bigger than her. It's a shame we don't have a fireplace actually, because we would never be short of firewood.'

'She's so funny. Her favourite thing is bunny-hopping through piles of dried leaves. It's like she's trying to pounce on a mouse or something, but I've never seen a mouse there. I think she's just pretending. She loves it when there's something real to chase too – she's a typical terrier. She bounds after squirrels, pheasants, anything. Sometimes she'll even get her lead between her little teeth and shake it like a rat!'

Most of the time though, Snowy stays very close to Mandy. 'She's a people pup,' she says. 'When I'm out walking with her, she will turn around all the time to see I'm still there. I call it "checking in". When she checks in you have to bend down and make a fuss of her, or she refuses to leave you alone. She will tangle her little body around your feet and literally trip you up if you don't give her a stroke. But as soon as you do, she'll trot along by your side with her stick, as happy as can be.'

Snowy's vocabulary has extended too. For most dogs, the word 'walkies' triggers great excitement and bouncing up and down with glee, and for Snowy it is no different. But instead of saying the word, Mandy looks at her puppy and swings her arms by her sides like she's walking. 'Snowy nearly turns herself inside out wagging her tail and runs down the stairs,' says Mandy. 'She gets all excited and pleased with herself when you give her the thumbs-up sign, but she also knows that a

wagging finger means she's done something naughty.

'She knows that if you hold something tasty between your finger and thumb and hold three fingers up on the other hand, then that's a special treat. She sits down and takes it very graciously.'

So Snowy has no problem getting by in the world, or communicating with her owner. 'Of course, I'm careful where I let her off the lead because she can't hear any dangers like traffic,' Mandy says. 'But in some ways Snowy's deafness is actually a good thing. Georgie used to be absolutely terrified of loud noises, like fireworks or guns being fired in the woods. But since she's lived with Snowy, who obviously isn't bothered in the least, she feels reassured and has calmed down a lot.'

Snowy loves a nice warm shower and then being blow-dried afterwards. Of course many dogs can be startled by the sound of a hairdryer, but Snowy knows nothing but the lovely hot air in her fur.

'And she can sleep through anything!' says Mandy. 'So really, having a deaf dog is no different. We talk to each other just fine. And every time I see how happy just a little thumbs-up signal makes her, I think to myself again that Snowy is perfect exactly as she is.'

An African wolf dog known as the basenji is the only dog in the world that cannot bark.

Dry food contains less water than tinned or moist food. So if you feed your dog only dry food make sure you give him lots of clean fresh water too.

If never spayed or neutered, a female dog, her mate and their puppies could produce over 66,000 dogs in six years!

The world's smallest dog breed is the chihuahua. Like human babies, chihuahuas are born with a soft spot in their skull that closes as they get older.

Dogs were the first animals to be domesticated by people, around 12,000 years ago.

Rhys is my Hear-o!

Woof woof, Poppy here.

Now that you've met Snowy and seen how dedicated some owners can be when their dog has a disability, it's time to introduce Rhys. I thought I would tell you his story to show that dogs can be just as passionate about making their owners' lives easier.

What sort of pooch do you picture when you think of an assistance dog? Most people imagine a big, solid golden retriever or maybe a glossy labrador, marching proudly and sturdily alongside their owner. They see big, heavy paws, a long muzzle, and a long, floppy tongue to fit.

Most people do not picture a dog like Rhys!

But then again, just as we dogs are the most

dependable creatures you'll ever meet, we are also full of surprises.

Who would have thought that this little ball of fluff would go on to have such a serious and important job? Some people like to make fun of small dogs, and when they do, I laugh at *them* because they have obviously never met my friend Rhys.

He may have the cutest, fluffiest face you've ever seen, and he may only be knee-high to a leggy dog like me, but let me assure you – Rhys is a little dog with a very big job.

Prepare to be inspired!

All my wags,
Poppy xxx

'When we first saw a picture of Rhys, we couldn't believe it,' Amanda says. 'He was quite clearly a pekinese! And a very fluffy one at that. But we were told this little dog could really help my mum around the house.' Amanda searched for a hint of a smirk from the lady from Hearing Dogs but found none. 'So we stared at the picture again. Though he wasn't exactly what we'd imagined, he was adorable and we were told he could be a huge help to mum so we agreed to meet him.'

Amanda's mum Barbara is deaf, and she had been considering getting an assistance dog for some time. Simple tasks that many people don't think twice about are very difficult when you can't hear what's going on around you. 'Mum can't hear the doorbell, so when she's at home on her own she doesn't know when she's got a visitor or when the post has arrived,' says Amanda. 'Being deaf can also sometimes be quite dangerous because you can't hear things like smoke or fire alarms. We wanted to find a way to make sure Mum's home life was as comfortable and as safe as possible.'

So, while Barbara and Amanda, at home in Nottinghamshire, began to research the possibility of getting a little furry helper, it was a busy day as usual many miles away at Dogs Trust Harefield.

'It was the twenty-third of February when Rhys first came through Dogs Trust's doors,' says Lisa, the chief puppy carer at the charity's Harefield rehoming centre. 'I remember that day exactly because it was the day I met one of the most wonderful puppies I've ever known. Of course, in my job I meet loads of amazing pups, but Rhys was one of my all-time favourites.'

When Rhys's owners popped the tiny auburn-and-white ball of fluff on the counter at reception and said they didn't have time to look after him, Lisa was astounded. The couple had bought the little peke from a pet shop without really thinking about what a big commitment they were taking on, and after a couple of months they decided they didn't want to take care of him any more.

'Although it upsets me to see people behave so thoughtlessly, at least Rhys's owners brought him to Dogs Trust instead of just abandoning him in the street like some people do,' Lisa says. 'But they really should have thought more carefully about what owning a dog means before doing it. Both of them worked full time and Rhys was left on his own in the house for eight hours in the daytime, and four hours in the evening. He was only a baby – it's so cruel to leave pups alone for long periods like that.'

Lisa looked down at the tiny dog on the counter and couldn't help but smile. 'Rhys was this tiny fluffy bundle, with a squashed little nose and two eyes like black marbles blinking at me from somewhere inside the fuzz. You couldn't even really see his legs because they were so short and his fur was so long. He was the cutest thing I had ever seen – I don't know how his owners managed to walk away from him.'

Lisa stroked the puffy little pup and the tiniest pink tongue flicked out good-naturedly to lick her finger. 'He didn't seem stressed out in any way,' she says. Some of the fur at the back of Rhys waggled back and forth, which Lisa took to be his tail. She scooped him up and took him to the vet for the check-up that all dogs have when they come to Dogs Trust.

The vet had a good look at Rhys and concluded that he was a fit and healthy pekinese, probably about three and a half months old. It was remarkable, the vet said, that the young pup was so

Have you seen a cuter pup than deaf Snowy?

New Pups on the Block

Rhys: Fluffball and Professional Pekinese

HEARING DOG PUPPY

Rhys is my Hear-o!

happy and laid-back considering his lonely life so far.

But laid-back he was. 'I'd never seen such a chilled out little pup before,' Lisa says. 'Rhys settled into the puppy block straight away. He was super-friendly and made friends with all the other puppies easily, but at the same time there was something so calm about him. When all the others were hurtling about in the kennel, throwing themselves at each other, jumping around and generally being normal, hyperactive pups, Rhys didn't see the point! He was perfectly happy to sit in his bed and chew a toy.'

This wasn't to say he didn't take part in some games. 'Rhys loved the puppy slide,' Lisa says. 'At our rehoming centre we've got a special garden – an enclosed area next to the puppy block where we let all the young puppies run around and play in the fresh air. There's a special slide they can crawl up to the top of and then slide down. Once Rhys worked out how to use it, we couldn't get him off! He would totter up to the top and whoosh back down, over and over again. I think all his fur made him extra slidey!'

Although Rhys loved puppy games and all his canine chums, it was clear Rhys's favourite thing in the world was human company. 'He was really people-oriented, and overjoyed to be around anybody at all,' says Lisa. 'It worked both ways, though. Visitors to the puppy block would always make a beeline for Rhys, because he looked so sweet and fluffy. And he learned from a very young age that saying hello to people in his adorable doggy way would mean lots of cuddles. He knew he was cute, and he really worked it to get himself lots of attention.'

One of his favourite ways of spending time with people was allowing himself to be brushed. 'He would lap up any sort of attention, but especially adored a good grooming session,' Lisa says. 'He'd sit there happily for ages while he had all his knots combed out. Some dogs hate being brushed, but not Rhys.'

One morning, Lisa was giving all the pups on the block their breakfast. 'When I feed the puppies, I do a little bit of training with them and try to get them to sit,' she says. 'I do that by holding a treat and waiting with it, then as soon as their bum touches the floor, I give them the treat. And then when they make the connection between sitting down and getting a treat, I start doing the same thing at meal times when I give them their food bowl.'

Lisa noticed that morning how much Rhys loved his food. 'He was amazing,' she says. 'A real pleasure to train. His natural desire to please people, combined with his love of eating made him the perfect student! He seemed to understand almost straight away what I wanted him to do. I was thinking about how special this little dog was when suddenly a thought came to me.

'I wondered if Rhys had what it took to be an assistance dog.'

Dogs Trust work closely with the charity Hearing Dogs for Deaf People and so are always on the lookout for new doggy recruits to help people who can't hear to live happier lives. 'I called our contact Liz and told them about our possible canine candidate,' Lisa says. 'She said he sounded fantastic and came to see him the very next day.'

Hearing Dogs for Deaf people recruit dogs from lots of places, including breeders and members of the public, and the charity also has its own breeding scheme. But whenever possible, the dogs are selected from rescue centres, to give abandoned pooches the chance to be valued and much-loved companions.

'Rhys was exactly the sort of pup we want,' Liz says. 'It doesn't matter if a dog is small or large, mongrel or pedigree, scruffy or sleek, the first thing we look for is good hearing, so we do lots of tests with a squeaky toy to see if their ears are up to the job. We also want dogs who are very friendly, confident and reliable in a variety of situations. It's great if they love their food or toys because that means we can use those things to motivate them. Rhys was perfect.'

So Lisa shed a tear as Liz swept the little peke away to begin his training, but felt happy about the important life that awaited him as a hearing dog. 'Hearing Dogs is a wonderful organisation,' she says. 'I knew Rhys would be adored and taken care of through his training and in his new home'.'

Liz says, 'After we select a dog, we take him to one of our volunteer socialisers, who gets him out and about and builds up his confidence. Once he is well-socialised and we think he's ready, the real training begins. We do four months of very positive training, reinforced with lots of praise and treats.

'First of all, we teach them to alert us to sounds. Depending on the size of the dog they alert in different ways. A little dog like Rhys "scrabbles", which means he jumps up and moves his little

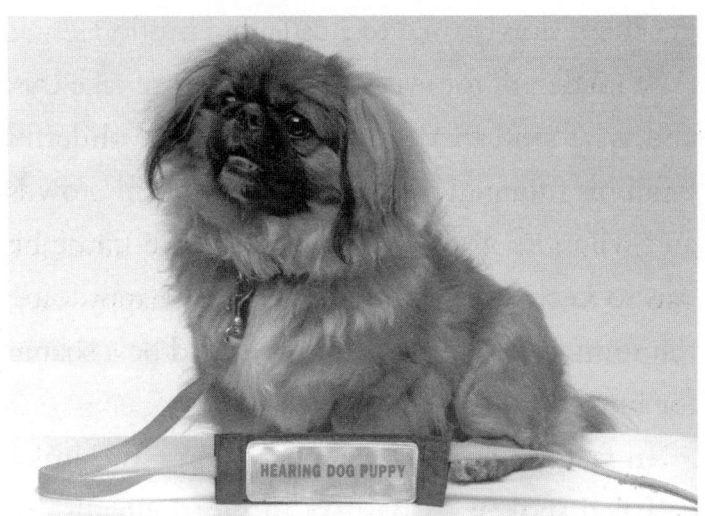

paws back and forth on the person. A medium-sized dog is trained to sit and put two paws on the person, and a large dog only places one paw.

'After that we teach them to lead us to sounds. Dogs and trainers get into pairs for that bit, and the dogs love it. It's really exciting for them, like a game.

'We spend lots of time in parks teaching them recall and getting them well-socialised with other dogs. And then we begin to take them into public places, like garden centres then shops and cafés, to get them slowly used to hustle and bustle.

'It's different for every dog how far we take this, and we found that though Rhys was wonderful in all his training, he was a bit nervous in crowds and when he was out and about. But because he was so keen and enthusiastic when he was doing the sound work, we thought it would be a shame for him to stop.

'In fact, we knew the perfect owner for him!

'I had spoken to Barbara in Nottinghamshire lots of times and I knew she was looking for a companion dog,' Liz says. 'She wanted a dog who would be her ears for her at home, alerting her to things that she needed to know. But when they were out together, she wanted that dog to just be a normal pet.'

'My mum thought she would find it a bit too much to have to take a dog absolutely everywhere with her, like on buses, into shops and so on,' Barbara's daughter Amanda says. 'Mum's in her seventies now and finds it difficult enough to get around herself without the extra responsibility of looking after a dog too. But she really wanted a doggy helper at home. So Liz introduced us to Rhys.'

Barbara had always thought of herself as a cat person, so was sceptical at first of what she thought looked like a little lap dog, but when they met, Rhys proved he was far more than that. 'Liz brought him round and Mum was charmed straight away,' says Amanda with a smile. 'Rhys was so sweet and relaxed, and he pottered about the house inquisitively, wagging his tail and seeming really interested and intelligent.'

Once Liz had assessed what Barbara needed from her hearing dog, she took Rhys away for lots more special training. Hearing Dogs even made a replica of Barbara's home to train Rhys in!

'He came back to the house two months later and stayed for the weekend so he and Mum could get to know each other better,' Amanda says. 'The two of them bonded really quickly. Rhys was so good. He was beautifully obedient, with a lovely nature and the cutest little face in the world.'

The following week the trainer from Hearing Dogs came round every day to work with Barbara and Rhys together, and the training went really well.

'The thing Mum needed alerting to most was the doorbell,' Amanda says. 'Before she had Rhys, she had a sort of doorbell that would make the lights in the house flash on and off instead of making a ringing noise. But sometimes cheeky children would come and push the button just to see all the lights inside flashing, and that made Mum feel nervous and vulnerable.

'But now she's got Rhys, she just has an ordinary doorbell, which she much prefers. When Rhys hears it ring, he runs over to Mum and scrabbles, then he sits down in front of her. She then asks him, "What is it?" Because Mum's deafness is the kind that means she can't hear or speak either, she communicates with hand signals.

The signal Rhys understands as "What is it?" is putting both hands in front of her, palms up. When she does that, Rhys leads her to the door and waits patiently, knowing he'll get a little treat.

'When he hears the smoke alarm or the fire alarm, he goes and scrabbles, but when she asks "What is it?" he lies flat so she knows he has heard something that means danger.

'If Mum's in bed and needs alerting to something, Rhys jumps up on to the bed, then he jumps off and waits for her to sit up and ask "What is it?" before telling her what he's heard. Because he's only got short legs, he has to give it a really big jump to get up there, but he knows it's important so he gives it all he's got!

'Rhys is very good at his job, partly because he loves his treats, but mostly I think because he loves Mum and he loves working. We have to do practice training every couple of weeks with him, where we show him different sounds and check he will still alert Mum in the right way, and he absolutely adores it! His whole body wags with excitement as he shows off what he can do.'

Perhaps the loveliest thing about the relationship between humans and dogs is that when the two species live together, they have the ability to understand each other on an intuitive level. So even though Rhys had special training to communicate important messages to Barbara, when the two got to know each other, Rhys began to understand other things that his owner needed too.

'He has a wonderful instinct for understanding Mum and helping her however he can,' says Amanda. 'Last winter, Mum became really ill with bronchitis. She had a terrible cough and at first Rhys was really nervous because he hadn't experienced her being like that before. But as soon as he understood she was poorly, he never ever left her side. Even if she had to get up in the middle of the night to get some medicine, Rhys would wake up too, follow her downstairs, wait for her, then follow her back up to bed before going back to sleep.

'He has also learned that Mum doesn't have very good balance, so unless he is leading her somewhere, he will walk behind her to make sure he doesn't trip her up! He's especially careful on the stairs.'

When Rhys is out in the park and off the lead he is trained to respond to a whistle instead of to his name, because Barbara can't shout. 'Sometimes he's a bit cheeky when I or my husband blow the whistle,' Amanda says. 'But never with Mum! He knows she's the boss and he's extremely loyal to her. In fact he will only go so far before turning around and looking for her, always making sure they're never too far apart.'

But as well as being a very dedicated worker, Rhys has a mischievous streak too, and loves to let his fur down and have fun. 'He loves getting grubby, and especially enjoys bounding through the snow or big muddy puddles,' says Amanda.

'But because he's got such little legs, sometimes he gets absolutely covered in mud. I remember once he threw himself into what he thought was an ordinary muddy puddle, but it turned out to be more of a bog. He leapt in and immediately vanished! And when he came out he was covered from head to toe in stinky mud!

'Mum always keeps a towel by the door to wipe his muddy paws when he gets back from his walks,' says Amanda. 'And when he's feeling silly, he'll get the towel and run off with it wagging his tail like crazy. Sometimes my husband grabs the other end of the towel and plays tug of war with him. Rhys adores that game! In fact, it's the only time he ever growls. Hearing dogs are trained not to bark or growl because they need to understand that they won't be heard. But we think Rhys forgets who he is when he's playing with his towel, and thinks he's a massive rottweiler instead!'

But he never forgets for long. 'Rhys loves coming for walks with me and my husband because he can have some proper time off work to be a normal carefree dog, but when it's time to go home, he can never wait to get back to Mum. He's absolutely devoted to her, and to his work.

'Hearing Dogs for Deaf People still support Mum and Rhys, and will keep supporting them for their whole life together.

'Rhys has brought Mum so much pleasure and company. She wishes she had applied for a companion dog years ago. He gives her confidence, unconditional love and complete loyalty. When people remark on how good he is, she feels like a proud parent!

'He may be little but he's a huge help in Mum's life and we all love him to bits.'

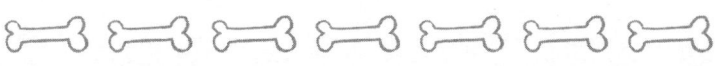

A dog's hearing is much better than a human's, especially for high-pitched sounds. If a dog suddenly pricks up his ears and becomes alert for no apparent reason, he might have detected bat or rodent sounds that we humans can't hear.

Television's original Lassie was actually a male dog.

According to ancient art, dogs have been wearing collars ever since Egyptian times!

Dogs that are left alone for long periods howl because they are lonely. In the wild, dogs howl to gather their pack around them. It's a type of bonding experience, and it's also useful so the pack can face dangerous situations together.

All dogs have 321 bones in their body.

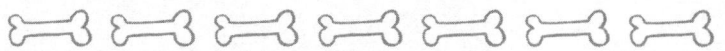

Otto's Tale of Wags to Riches

Lick, lick, wag, wag.

When I tell people I'm writing a book of stories about puppies, lots of them wonder what on earth I'm writing. 'But puppies are too young to have *done* anything!' they exclaim. 'They're born, they're cute and they, er, chew things. Surely that's it?'

Some people really are baffled.

But little do they know that in nine short months a puppy can experience an epic adventure, complete with twists and turns, mystery, crime, intrigue, and even a fairytale ending.

In fact Otto's story is so great, I wouldn't be surprised if Disney come along soon asking for the rights to make a movie. (I would have to make a cameo appearance, naturally.)

135

So move along *Marley*, and make way for Otto!
Remember, you met him here first!

Nuzzles,

Pops xxx

There has been a castle at the site of Chilham, on the edge of a wood in the Kent countryside, for at least thirteen centuries. Today the magnificent house is home to the Wheeler family – Tessa, Stuart, their three daughters Sarah Rose, Jacquetta and Charlotte, and a nine-month-old lurcher, Otto.

To see this young dog now, king of the castle in all his brindle glory, you would never believe what he had been through in his first few months of life.

Otto's story begins with Munchie and Pickles, two twelve-week-old lurcher pups found straying and brought by a member of the public to Dogs Trust Evesham. Munchie was a male pup with a beautiful rough brindle coat, and Pickles was his sister, who had smooth black-and-white fur.

'Just like normal little pups, they settled into rehoming centre life very easily,' says Tracy, the canine carer on the puppy block. 'They were playful, excitable, sweet and a joy to be around. They both loved the company of people and other dogs and couldn't get enough of their toys.'

Munchie was the more outgoing of the two. 'He used to grab people's trousers with his little teeth,' laughs Tracy. 'And sometimes their skin too, which was a bit naughty. He loved knees especially! He was only playing though – he was a really affectionate puppy and would never want to hurt anybody.'

Tracy tried to get Munchie out of the knee-nipping habit by showing him the game tug o' war with a rag pull, which he took to very enthusiastically. He had a wide little face and a strong jaw – evidence of some bull breed in the pups' family.

One evening, as normal, Tracy was getting all the puppies ready for bed. She fed them their dinner, made sure their kennels were clean, and pulled down all the hatches which lead out into the enclosed outside area. Munchie and Pickles were playing as usual, tumbling over each other happily in their kennel when Tracy closed the door and left for the night.

The next morning, as soon as she walked into the puppy block, she knew that something was wrong. The pups yapped at her excitedly for attention and breakfast. She heard all voices except two. Tracy walked over to Munchie and Pickles' kennel and gasped.

The little lurchers were gone.

'I couldn't believe it. I knew straight away that we had a robbery on our hands,' Tracy says. 'Munchie and Pickles's outside hatch was ajar. It was clear that someone had jumped over the back

wall to the rehoming centre and entered the puppy block through the hatch. The thieves must have been very determined to go to so much trouble, because even getting to the back wall of the centre through the private fields would have been tricky.

'We think the robbery happened early in the night, because you can tell when a dog's bed has been slept in. Munchie and Pickles' blankets were still smooth and looked just like they did when I'd laid them out the night before.'

All the staff were devastated. They were angry that anyone could do something so horrible. But most of all, they were desperately worried about the two helpless little dogs. Anyone who would steal from a rescue charity would be unlikely to be a good dog owner, they thought grimly.

Munchie and Pickles were in deep trouble, everyone was sure of that.

The police were called, who filed a report, and Dogs Trust started a big campaign to find the puppies. 'We called the two local newspapers, who both wrote big articles with pictures of the stolen pups,' Tracy says. 'And we put posters up absolutely everywhere — all round the town centre, in vets', pet shops, everywhere we could think of. The community were very supportive. We just wanted to know Munchie and Pickles were safe, and for them to come back so we could find them proper new homes with owners who would love them.'

But despite everyone's efforts, the trail was cold. Nobody seemed to know who had committed the terrible crime, and after a while, Tracy and the rest of the staff began to lose hope that the puppies would ever be found.

Rehoming centre life had to continue as normal. And as time passed in the town, the posters started coming down and people in shops and at bus stops stopped talking about the two stolen puppies. The centre increased its security by making sure every possible entrance and hatch was fitted with a lock so there was no chance of it happening again.

Five busy months passed, and then one Tuesday in March, some news came in that was so amazing nobody could quite believe it.

One hundred and seventy-one miles away in Dartford in Kent, a young brindle lurcher had been found wandering stray in a hospital car park. He was taken to the local dog warden who scanned him for a microchip and immediately identified him.

The dog warden called the nearest Dogs Trust rehoming centre, in Canterbury, and told them who he'd found.

It was Munchie!

After calling Dogs Trust Evesham with the news, the manager rushed out to pick him up. 'Poor Munchie seemed very quiet and shocked when he first came into the centre,' says Nico, the puppy carer in Canterbury. 'We were all so happy he'd been found, even though we knew his sister was still out there somewhere.'

Munchie had obviously grown since the last time Dogs Trust had seen him, and didn't look much like his puppy photos anymore. 'He was really out of proportion,' Nico says, with a grin. 'It was as if he hadn't quite grown into his body parts yet. We were expecting a slender, fragile whippet-type dog, and instead we had this bulky little creature who looked ready to take on the world! He was really handsome though, with lovely eyes.'

As Munchie relaxed and began to come out of his shell, Nico began to get a better idea of the sort of life he'd been living. 'He wasn't exactly afraid of people, but he wasn't happy to see them like a well cared-for dog would be,' Nico says. 'It seemed like whoever had owned him hadn't treated him like a pet. He'd been owned more like you would own a piece of luggage or a sofa or something.

'In himself, he was a happy dog but he clearly hadn't been shown any love or affection by humans in the time he'd been missing. It seemed as if he'd spent most of his time in doggy company, and so he looked to other dogs for his comfort and fun.'

Staff did lots of positive training with him, piling on loads of praise and encouragement every time he got something right. 'As he got to know a person, he was all over them,' laughs Nico. 'He was like a mad thing, wagging his tail like crazy and kissing them. It was clear he wanted that human love he'd been missing out on, and because he was still a baby we were able to restore his faith in people relatively easily.'

'The main thing we really had to work on was lead training, lead training, lead training! Munchie really was a live wire. It was like he'd get a fly in his pants, and he was off, whether he was off the lead or on it! He would get a special look in his eye, his ears would twitch back and he would *run*. He'd stick his bum underneath him like a proper lurcher and his back legs would almost overtake his front legs. If he happened to be on the lead, he'd get to the end of it then he'd get neck burn and we'd get rope burn. It was awful!'

But with a harness instead of a collar, and two weeks of love, attention and gravy bones as treats, Munchie was walking perfectly on his lead. 'It would usually take a lot longer than that,' Nico says. 'Munchie was special though. He was a really eager, smashing little dog.'

And once he'd properly settled into life at the rehoming centre, he was a puppy again. He had a cheeky, inquisitive character and loved any kind of toy. He amused himself with squeaky toys, fluffy toys and especially old socks. 'Some of our supporters bring us old socks to roll into balls for the dogs to play with,' says Nico. 'Munchie used to like unravelling one, holding it by its end and flipping it back and forth around his face.'

Munchie's story was displayed proudly in the centre, with an article and photo cut out of the local paper and a map showing the one hundred and seventy-one miles he had travelled since he went missing from Dogs Trust Evesham.

The chirpy young dog began to attract more and more attention from potential rehomers as he larked about in his kennel with his kennelmate. He was booked to go to a new home once but sadly it fell through when the person changed their mind at the last minute. And then one day Tessa, owner of the huge and magnificent Chilham Castle, came to Dogs Trust Canterbury.

'I'd always had dogs in the past,' she says, 'and I particularly like lurchers. But at that time we were dogless. It was our youngest daughter Charlotte who was the most keen for us to get another, and all three of our children said how sad it was to come home with no dog to greet them.'

Very much a believer in rehoming rescue dogs, Tessa visited her local Dogs Trust rehoming centre. 'Quickly, I could tell which of our residents Tessa was most interested in,' says Nico. 'We talked about a few different dogs, but she kept coming back to Munchie. So we took him out for a walk together to see how they got on. He was adorable and enthusiastic as always. He did play up a little bit and seemed to love the taste of her shoes because he kept licking them, but Tessa didn't seem to mind.'

'He ticked all the boxes for me,' says Tessa. 'He was such a handsome dog. He was young and full of beans with a lovely character. And, actually quite an important characteristic for us, he had short fur. There's a big lake in the castle's grounds that all dogs seem to love jumping into, and dealing with long, muddy fur on a regular basis would be a nightmare.'

So Tessa went away to talk to her family and think long and hard about whether rehoming another dog would be the right thing to do. And, after another visit to Munchie with her daughters, they all decided:

Yes!

Munchie would be a wonderful addition to the

family and the castle. Tessa's daughter Charlotte thought, after all the little dog had been through, he deserved a new beginning and a new name. And after much deliberation, Otto was chosen.

After all the checks had been done, the paperwork filled in and Otto's microchip updated with his new name and his impressive new address, the eight-month old lurcher finally went to his forever home – the splendid, centuries-old Chilham Castle set in three hundred acres of elegant parkland with even its own helicopter landing space!

It is obviously lovely for a dog to be living in such a huge house with so much beautiful space to explore, but there are a few challenges as well. 'Otto can be pretty wild and energetic,' says Tessa. 'And because the castle is so big, we can't let him in to the vast majority of it. He has managed to escape into some of our grand wood-panelled reception rooms before and he's wreaked complete havoc. And it's the same with the gardens really. Otto doesn't really care about the stunning views of the North Downs or Canterbury Cathedral – he just loves getting muddy! He's so enthusiastic he really does have to be supervised at all times.'

Otto's typical day is quite a dream one for a dog, however. Carleton, the chef at Chilham Castle and Tessa's 'deputy dog owner', takes the chirpy lurcher out very early in the morning for a run around the lake, which is so enormous that it's open for visitors to arrange fishing trips on it.

When they come back, Otto has his breakfast and a lounge around in his own special room in the castle, where his bed and all his toys are kept. (How many dogs can boast their own stately living quarters?) Then, when he's had a snooze, Tessa takes him out for another walk. He'll follow her up a big staircase to her studio and play with a chew while she works, and then they go down to the stables together to see to the horses. 'He loves coming to the stables but I have to keep him

on his lead away from the horses,' Tessa says, 'or he causes all sorts of trouble!'

After that, they go to see Ali, the event manager at the castle. A range of special events are held at Chilham Castle; from poker parties to big canapé receptions to summer entertaining in the beautiful, octagonal, grassed courtyard. And Ali has a lively dalmatian called Theo. 'Otto and Theo get on like a house on fire,' says Tessa. 'They'll run around and play together for hours, which makes Otto nice and exhausted for the evening! I give him his dinner and a final walk and that's the end of his day.

'He's only been with us for a couple of months but he's really enjoying life here at the castle,' says Tessa. 'He's been a bit of a challenge to housetrain and sometimes doesn't understand the difference between outside and inside where that's concerned. But we're getting there. I think it's because of how he was treated by whoever stole him. We're doing lots of training sessions with him to teach him the lessons he should have learned in those missing months.'

He still loves to grab at people's clothing when he gets excited, just like he did when he was a tiny puppy. This is a problem that Tessa and his trainers are working on, but it means he isn't allowed to meet castle guests. 'Otto has a very sweet character and his clothes-snatching is a purely friendly gesture, but can you imagine if he grabbed at a lady's silk dress?' Tessa says. 'It would be a disaster!'

So even though Otto is the same dog with the same funny little ways, it just goes to show how much things can change in one puppy's life. To go from homeless to kidnapped to lord of the manor in just a few months really is astonishing. All credit goes to Otto's microchip – without which things may not have turned out so well for the stripy young dog. 'If he wasn't microchipped we would never have found him,' says Nico. 'I think it should be made compulsory for owners to chip their dogs. It's so much better to have a microchip and not need it than to not have one and lose your dog for ever.

'Sadly Otto's sister Pickles is still out there somewhere. But we know that if she is ever found straying or gets lost again, the details on her microchip will lead her straight back to us. And we will never give up hope.'

153

The oldest known breed is the saluki, originally trained by Egyptians to help them track game.

Dogs have twice as many muscles for moving their ears as humans do.

Dogs don't lose heat quickly by sweating from their whole bodies like people do. Instead they cool down by panting, which removes heat from their bodies through the surface of the tongue. Dogs also pant when they are nervous or excited.

Up until the late 1800s, collies were known as Scottish sheepdogs.

Nearly all dogs have pink tongues, except the chow chow and the shar-pei, who both have black tongues.

Elvis: A Little Legend

Hello readers.

I've often noticed how people love to make comparisons between dogs and humans. A lookey-likey competition is even one of the main events in most dog shows! With my long legs and fine bone structure, lots of people have said I'm the spitting image of Kate Moss. And when I'm running, others have said they could easily mistake me for Paula Radcliffe.

Our next puppy has a superstar lookey-likey too. In fact, he bears a startling resemblance to one of the most famous human beings of the twentieth century. With his very recognisable face and curled lip, Elvis looks like, you guessed it, Elvis Presley!

In this next tale of abandonment, challenges and

new beginnings, all Elvis needed was a caring owner to love him tender and make his dreams come true.

I hope you enjoy meeting this remarkable pup, because to have been through so much and still have such a sunny nature, one thing's for sure: Elvis really is a little legend.

Lots of licks,

Pops xxx

Like many other unwanted puppies, young Elvis came into Dogs Trust Merseyside in a cardboard box. He and his four sisters were only six weeks old when their owner decided that he didn't want to look after them, even though puppies should be at least eight weeks before they are taken away from their mother. But the five new arrivals were welcomed into the rehoming centre and made as cosy as possible in the puppy block.

At that time, Caroline and her partner Paula were working at the centre as volunteers. Dogs Trust is very lucky to have wonderful volunteers who work tirelessly for the dogs in its care. These amazing people do not work for money; they do it just because they love dogs so much and want to help in whatever way they can.

'One day Paula and I arrived at the centre to start work,' Caroline says. 'And to our joy, we were asked to spend some time socialising a litter of puppies. Socialising means a lot of playing – getting the pups used to people and teaching them how to enjoy human company. Of course we jumped at the chance, because who doesn't love playing with puppies?

'We went into the play area, which was a big, grassy enclosure full of toys and surrounded by trees. A puppy carer approached us with a big grin on her face and a tiny pup under each arm, and another carer was carrying a bundle of three more. They put the puppies down on the grass and left us to play with them. So we sat down and to our delight, the puppies immediately jumped all over us, tumbling around excitedly.

'There were four beautiful females with glossy

black fur and one little brown male. He was only about a third of his sisters' size, and when we saw him we couldn't believe how cute and adorable he was,' says Caroline, 'He was like the little lost boy. The girl pups bullied him constantly. They kept pushing him over boisterously and barking at him, but he had such a sweet, gentle nature. He really tried hard to join in with their games, but they kept pushing him away. It was heartbreaking to watch.'

Elvis's body was exceptionally soft and wrinkly. 'It looked as though his skin was too big for him,' says Caroline. 'But one terribly striking thing was that he looked as if he had a big hole in the middle of his face.' What Elvis actually had was a hair lip and cleft palate. This is a birth defect that people can suffer from too, where the upper lip is split open up to the nostril. The condition made his little face look very unusual indeed. His teeth showed through the gap, which made him appear quite ferocious, if you didn't know him and that

he was actually as gentle as a puppy could be.

Apart from his appearance, Elvis's condition also meant that he couldn't bark, but only make funny little growling noises. He also couldn't eat properly, as the food kept coming out of his mouth and dribbling down his furry face. He always needed special care at feeding time. 'Every morsel of food had to be mashed up and fed to him by hand in case it went through the gap and into his lungs, which could have killed him,' says Caroline.

But in spite of his sad deformity, Elvis had a spirited personality and was always ready for mischief and games when his sisters gave him the chance. Caroline and Paula became more and more attached to the wonky little pup and he soon became a firm favourite with all the staff at the rehoming centre.

Everyone agreed they should name him Elvis because his little lip curled up like the King of Rock 'n' Roll himself. The name also suited the little dog because he had so much energy that he seemed to bounce happily through life. 'He had a real star's personality,' says Caroline fondly.

The weeks passed, and by now the pups were old enough to go to new homes. People started to arrive and admire the four beautiful sisters with their glossy coats and sparkling eyes. One by one they were taken away to be cared for by loving owners. Finally just one remained – Elvis.

'We knew that he would have to have surgery on his face when he was old enough,' says

Caroline. 'And staff at the centre were worried about rehoming him when there were no guarantees that he would survive his condition or the operation either. But he didn't know. He just carried on feeling the joy of life and the fun of games and the marvellous pleasure of a good chewy bone.'

The upbeat little puppy loved Caroline and Paula's company, and they were finding more and more that they missed him when he wasn't around. 'We had no intention of getting a dog, let alone a puppy,' says Caroline. 'But after a few weeks of knowing Elvis, and lots of thought and long conversations about how our lives would change if we became dog owners, we found ourselves desperately wanting to take him home with us.'

One thing was for certain – Elvis would need a lot of care. But his wonderful spirit and his wonky face had worked their magic on Caroline and Paula and they both agreed that he was the only

Uh-huh, it's wonky but wonderful Elvis!

From wags as Munchie ...

... to riches as Otto!

Tiny Tim, the abandoned Christmas pup

Tiny Tim poses with his toys

dog for them. 'I think deep down we knew we were going to be taking that puppy home no matter what,' laughs Caroline.

Elvis was no sooner settled and happy with his new family, when fame came knocking on the door. 'He had a very exciting first few months as he was chosen as the Dogs Trust Valentine dog,' says Caroline proudly. Despite the strangeness of his face, his personality shone through and now no one could help but love him. Like any star he had to deal with a lot of publicity and photo shoots, and when the photographs were released he became a local celebrity. Everyone wanted to stop him in the park for a word and a cuddle, and he couldn't get enough of all the attention.

Elvis shared his home with two cats, Frobisher and Ginni. While Ginni had no time for playful puppies, Frobisher and Elvis became great friends. They would take turns to chase each other, tearing around the house at top speed, then end up snuggled together on the sofa, and Elvis would wash the cat's ears with vigorous licks. Sometimes Frobisher would not be in the mood for games, and would bat Elvis over the head with his paw, but the next minute all would be forgotten as they charged around the house after each other again.

Gone were the days when Elvis was the victim of bullies. He now had a wide circle of doggy friends who he played with at the park. Archie, a huge long-haired German shepherd was his best pal, who in spite of his size, was happy to let Elvis reach up and lick his face affectionately. Lily the collie-cross never minded sharing her toys with him, and Nero the Rhodesian ridgeback was a great friend too. Often there were up to twenty dogs in the park at once all having a wonderful time, and Elvis was always right in the middle of it.

At five and a half months, it was time to think about the operation to correct the split in the young dog's mouth. Caroline and Paula took him to Manchester to see a specialist vet who would

Elvis is a Legend

carry out the surgery. It was a complicated operation and involved removing badly placed teeth and repairing his cleft palate and hair lip. At the same time the vet had to create a new nostril where it had been missing. 'Elvis went in as a dog with a hole in his face, and came out looking just slightly wonky,' Caroline says. 'But he had always been handsome to us.'

Just two days after his operation, Elvis was back to his usual bouncy, waggy self. 'It was amazing,' says Caroline. 'After just forty-eight hours, it was like nothing had happened. Emotionally, he had an unbelievably quick recovery, but we had to remember that he had stitches in his palate, nose and mouth. He badly wanted to roll around with Frobisher, to play rough with his friends in the park and to chew on his favourite hide bones, but for six weeks we had to be so careful not to let anything knock his face. That was really hard on him. But when those final stitches came out and we let him off the lead in the park for the first time in weeks, he was overjoyed! It was like he was saying *Yippeeeee!* as he ran round and round the park with his friends. It was a joy to watch him that day.'

But sadly, Elvis's health issues didn't end when those final stitches were removed. One day, months later, Caroline was working at the rehoming centre when there was a message over the radio telling her to come to reception because Paula was on the phone. 'I had a terrible feeling something was wrong so I dropped everything and ran to the phone,' says Caroline. 'Paula was at home in tears, saying that she thought Elvis had just had a fit. I turned to my manager who told me I must go home straight away. So I rushed back and we took Elvis to the vet's immediately. They were fantastic – I couldn't have asked for Elvis to be cared for by calmer, more helpful people.'

The vet said that Elvis's fit could possibly have been a one-off, because on rare occasions that happens to dogs. But they told her to watch the poor dog carefully, because the fits could mean he has epilepsy. And sure enough, within the next two days, Elvis had a further four or five epileptic fits.

'Humans and dogs can both suffer from epilepsy, and it's very scary seeing someone have a fit,' Caroline says. 'Some dogs really thrash around a lot when it's happening. Elvis acts a bit differently, but it's still awful. Just before he has a fit, he comes and leans against me as if he's trying to say something is wrong. Then he slides down to the ground and I end up kneeling on the floor with him, supporting his head so he doesn't hurt himself. Then he becomes very distant for a minute or two, his legs twitch and his whole body goes stiff. And then very slowly he comes back.

'When he emerges from a fit he is absolutely ravenous! Dogs often behave strangely for a while after a fit. He will eat and eat and eat if you let him – it's incredible.'

The vet checked Elvis thoroughly and told Caroline and Paula that the epilepsy could be controlled with tablets. And though Elvis still experiences some bad fits, he is much better. He now takes ten tablets a day, but he doesn't mind too much as Caroline lovingly wraps each one in his favourite processed cheese. 'We call it cheesy snack time,' laughs Caroline.

Now, a couple of years on, Caroline works for Dogs Trust as a permanent member of staff and Elvis comes to work with her occasionally, but he really prefers staying at home with Paula. He's a lovely, snuggly dog who likes to sleep late under his fleecy blanket, to chase around with all his pals in the park, and to soak up the sun in the garden.

'We never ever leave him alone, in case he has a fit when we're not there,' Caroline says. 'If we ever have to go somewhere without him, we make sure we get a dogsitter.

'But we don't mind that he needs so much care. In fact we feel very lucky to have him. He's such a friendly, happy dog despite his problems. He has loads of doggy and human friends, including all the vets, nurses and reception staff who know and love him. And he's so much fun too. He's got a really cheeky streak!'

One of Elvis's favourite games is pinching things out of people's pockets and running off with them. 'It started when Paula's dad was sitting at the kitchen table doing a crossword, and there was a handkerchief hanging out of his pocket,' says Caroline. 'Elvis suddenly decided the hanky looked fun, so he grabbed it and ran off outside with it. When Paula's dad saw him, he ran after the dog and started chasing him around the garden. Well of course, to Elvis, that was an instant game! So now anything that's hanging out of a pocket is snatched immediately. We have to tell anyone who comes round and sits at the table to be careful! Tissues are his favourite thing. He bounces around the house tearing them up into a million tiny pieces, and leaving them everywhere.'

Only now, nearly two years after the operation on his mouth, is Elvis learning to bark – that simple doggy word that wasn't possible before because of the shape of his mouth. 'The first time I heard him bark it really made me jump!' Caroline says. 'He was running around playing with a friend of his – a little staffie called Crash. Crash was getting a bit boisterous and pinning Elvis down with his whole body, when suddenly there was this growl and a little *rrrrrrruff*! It was so strange to hear that sound coming from Elvis, who had only really made funny little groaning noises before that. Paula and I both love to see him learning normal doggy behaviour.

'Actually it's wonderful that Elvis is able to be a normal dog,' Caroline continues. 'If it weren't for Dogs Trust, he would realistically have very little chance of that. He is on a part-foster scheme, which means that the charity pays for any medical expenses that are related to his face, and it has now been extended to cover his epilepsy too. The vet bills would have run into thousands of pounds by now, and there is no way Paula and I could have afforded to pay them by ourselves.

'It's just amazing that there are so many dog lovers out there who make generous donations to Dogs Trust. And that money doesn't just help Elvis and thousands of others like him to live happy, healthy lives, it also allows me and Paula the privilege of owning the very best dog in the world!'

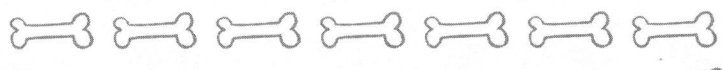

A dog's barking in the wild tells puppies to take cover and hide, and alerts the other dogs in the pack to assemble for action. Dogs also bark when they are excited, bored or stressed in some way.

Three dogs survived the sinking of the Titanic – a newfoundland, a pomeranian, and a pekinese.

A German shepherd can have as many as two hundred and twenty million 'smelling' cells in his nose, while a person has only five million.

The 'spring' in springer spaniel comes from their role as hunting dogs. They would make the birds they were hunting 'spring' into the air.

Puppies grow in their mother's belly for sixty to seventy days.

Tiny Tim's Christmas Tale

Lick lick, hello readers.

Paws up everyone who loves Christmas! I certainly do. For me, the festive season means spending lots of time with my favourite people and dearest dogs. It means turkey dinners, new toys, turkey scraps, Christmas trees, turkey leftovers, fun, games, and lovely juicy turkey. It means going for extra-long walks in the snow, and then coming back, exhausted and happy, to a cosy house, a warm rug and a nice turkey snack.

I really do love Christmas. But one thing I never forget is that this is the time of year when many of my less fortunate canine comrades suffer most. And the cause of this suffering, readers, is one very innocent-seeming thing. It may shock you to hear what it is, because lots of people actually think it's the best thing about Christmas. But for many helpless puppies, it really is the very worst. The wonderful but terrible thing is this:

Presents.

Now don't get me wrong – I love presents. Squeaky toys are amazing. And rag pulls. And a lovely chewy pig's ear is another favourite. In fact most presents are a wonderful idea, with a very important exception. Presents that are *alive* are a terrible idea. And even though we at Dogs Trust work hard to spread our message 'a dog is for life, not just for Christmas', year after year, people still buy puppies as presents without considering what a huge commitment they need from their owners. And year after year, these poor pooches are abandoned because the people they are bought for can't take care of them.

Sometimes they are taken to rescue centres like Dogs Trust, where staff will do their best to find them a proper home, but often they are just left outside where all they can do is try to survive on their own.

And you can imagine how hard that is as a tiny and terrified puppy in the middle of winter.

I'd like you to meet one such 'unwanted gift', who was found all alone, freezing in the Christmas snow at just nine weeks old. Here is the tale of Tiny Tim, one of the sweetest puppies you will ever see, and with a story to melt even the frostiest heart. I hope you'll love him as much as I do.

Wags and woofs,
Pops xxx

It was the day before Christmas Eve and Barry was freezing. He couldn't wait to get home. He loved his job in the summer, when he could stroll around Leeds in the sunshine. He would wear his special dog warden T-shirt and exchange cheerful hellos with all the local owners who were out enjoying the weather with their dogs. He'd even slurp the occasional ice cream while he patrolled the parks looking for lost or stray dogs to help. But in the middle of winter being a dog warden was a different story altogether. Spending all day in the frosty outdoors wasn't nearly as pleasant, and this winter was especially cold.

Apart from one or two owners throwing sticks for their dogs in the distance, the park was deserted and snow was falling fast. The green of the grass was turning into a bright sparkly white, and everything had that special stillness and silence that only comes when it's snowing.

Barry huddled his ears deeper into the collar of his coat. It was nearly the end of his shift and he was trying to distract himself from the icy flakes falling and melting on his face by thinking about dinner. *"Sausages or casserole?"* he thought to himself dreamily as he plodded in big steps through the snow on his way back to his van.

But just as the vehicle came into view, suddenly a stirring in the corner of his eye made him jump. He looked at the ground. There it was again. Under a bench, there was a faint little wriggle. He definitely hadn't imagined it. He walked over to where he saw the movement and stooped down to take a closer look.

Barry stared in astonishment into the snow as a

tiny black face with two shiny eyes blinked back up at him. He couldn't believe it. There in front of him was the smallest puppy he had ever seen in his life. He had short black, white and brown fur and was no bigger than the palm of Barry's hand. The warmth from the tiny dog had melted a bit of the snow around him and the poor creature was huddled into a ball on the pavement, his tail curled tightly underneath him and his tiny body visibly shaking with cold.

At first Barry wondered how such a pup could get lost when he was barely old enough to leave his mother. He looked around for any sign of an owner. There was nobody. Then he remembered. It was nearly Christmas. It's not usually until after Christmas that they begin to find abandoned puppies, but this little chap was most likely an early present, Barry thought to himself. And clearly an early present that the receiver did not want.

Barry unzipped his big coat, scooped up the

terrified little animal, and popped him inside to try and warm him up. The poor pup weighed almost nothing but Barry could feel the little body stiff with cold and fear, shivering inside his coat as he hurried back to the van.

'When I first saw that little puppy and Barry told me the story it broke my heart,' says Amanda, manager of Dogs Trust Leeds. 'He's a Jack Russell, but even for that breed he was absolutely tiny. And he was clearly very ill indeed. We rushed him straight to the vet suite.'

The vet was very concerned about the miniature pup and diagnosed him with hypothermia – a dangerous state that comes from being very cold for too long. He put him on a drip and placed him on a little heated pad to give him lots of warmth. The puppy was only about nine weeks old. He had a cough, and was very thin from lack of food. And having had no water for a long time too, he was extremely dehydrated. 'It was so lucky Barry found him because the vet said there was no way he would have lasted the night out there in the cold,' Amanda says. 'We decided to call him Tiny Tim, because of his size and because Tiny Tim is a character from the story *A Christmas Carol* and Christmas was fast approaching.'

Tiny Tim had none of the usual puppy energy and clearly needed lots of care to make him healthy again, so Amanda decided to take him home to live with her for a few days. She has two dogs and two cats of her own but all the animals seemed to understand Tiny Tim was ill and were kind and gentle with him. 'Both my cats were absolutely massive compared to him!' says Amanda. 'That's how small he was!

'He badly needed food but I had a terrible time getting him to eat because he was so starved. Eventually he began to take little bits, but then he would be sick because his stomach was so sensitive. I could only give him the tiniest amounts – literally a teaspoon of puppy food – at regular intervals.'

Christmas Day came and Amanda went to work, taking Tiny Tim with her in a carry case she had made cosy with warm blankets and his heated pad. Staff at Dogs Trust work hard to make sure the dogs at the rehoming centre have a special day at Christmas. They give them all new toys, take them for a lovely long walk and feed them a special turkey dinner. However Tiny Tim was too ill for any of those things, and just snuggled sadly and quietly in his box.

As staff went about their duties, and cheerful Christmas festive music played out across the rehoming centre, everyone remembered to stop by and give Tiny Tim a reassuring stroke. They popped a little fluffy reindeer next to him in his box too, to show they hadn't forgotten him.

At the end of the day, Amanda went home to have her own Christmas with her family, again taking the poor pooch with her. 'I was busy making the roast potatoes when all of a sudden I heard a sad whimpering coming from Tiny Tim,' she says. 'I rushed over to him and saw he was in so much pain that he was crying. His little stomach was badly bloated. It was as if he'd been blown up like a balloon. There was no way around it – I had to put Christmas dinner on hold and rush him back to the vet's.'

When they arrived, the vet diagnosed the whimpering pup with a bad case of trapped wind. He prescribed some pain relief and some anti-inflammatory medicine for his stomach. 'I felt so sorry for the little thing,' says Amanda. 'I even forgot it was Christmas Day for a while. When we eventually came home and got around to having our dinner Tiny Tim sat on my lap quietly through the whole meal. It was only afterwards, when we were having our Christmas pudding, that I could tell the vet's medicine had really helped. His little head started popping up at the table and he kept trying to get up amongst all the plates and say hello to everyone!'

By the end of the day, Tiny Tim was far happier

and a lovely puppyish personality began to shine through for the first time. 'He started to act really cheeky, just like puppies should be,' Amanda says. 'He was still very affectionate and would share himself around, moving from lap to lap, but he also began to show some interest in running about, wagging his little tail and wanting to play. It made everyone so happy to see the change in his character as he started to feel better.'

The next day was Boxing Day and Amanda was going away for a few days to visit some family. She badly didn't want to leave the little dog but her workmate Amy agreed that she would take over and be his temporary owner.

'I'd already spent lots of time with Tiny Tim since he'd been coming into work with Amanda,' Amy says. 'In fact all the staff at the centre adored him and made a huge fuss of him. He'd had such a horrible experience we all wanted to lavish him with as much love as we possibly could.

'Though he'd come on in leaps and bounds in

the three days that Amanda had been looking after him, when I took him to my house on Boxing Day he still couldn't eat properly, he still had his little cough, and he still wasn't as energetic and carefree as a puppy should be.'

But with every day that passed, Tiny Tim grew stronger and healthier. 'It was amazing to watch him getting better,' Amy says. 'By hand-feeding tiny amounts into his little mouth with a teaspoon, Amanda and I literally brought him back from the brink of death. I developed an incredibly strong bond with Tiny Tim because of this, and fell head over heels in love with him.'

Tiny Tim's puppy-like character grew day by day, as he became more outgoing and confident. 'He was so funny,' laughs Amy. 'His jaw was sort of overshot on the top, and when you called him he pulled a face which made him look like he was grinning at you. He became really cheeky too – running off with things he wasn't supposed to all the time. He'd always bring

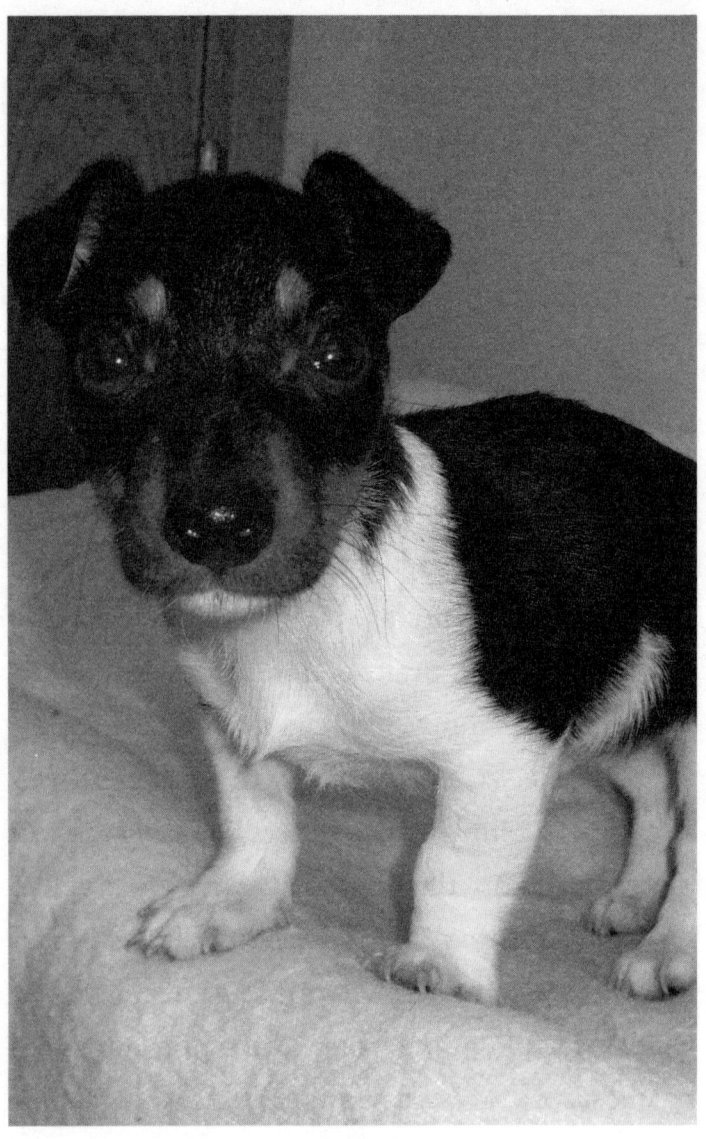

them back though. He was so sweet – he wanted to play but he didn't want to cause any trouble!

'He liked to give the TV a piece of his mind too. It seemed like he didn't quite understand it – sometimes he'd be a bit frightened of it if a sudden noise made him jump. And then other times he would yap happily along in unison with it, wagging his tail!

'As his health improved he made me laugh more and more with his sweet little ways. I couldn't bear the thought of giving him up, but I knew I had to. My other dog Ellie was quite elderly and could be a bit grumpy, and though she was tolerant of Tiny Tim, I knew she didn't want to share her home with the bouncy little puppy that he was becoming. And I see so many dogs in my job at Dogs Trust that I desperately want to adopt, I had to remind myself that Tiny Tim was just one of them. It's so hard not to fill my house with dogs, but finding happy homes for them with loving new owners is just as satisfying.'

Amy told herself she must be strong and that she could not be Tiny Tim's permanent owner. So after the New Year, when the little Jack Russell was at full strength, she began to look out for owners that would be suitable for the special little dog. Eventually along came a couple who she thought would be just perfect. They met Tiny Tim and loved him – all the more when they heard what he'd been through. They agreed enthusiastically that they could give him the home he needed to grow up into a happy, healthy dog.

So on the fourth of January, after his new owners had passed all the rehoming tests, Tiny Tim went to live with his overjoyed new owners, where he continues to be loved and looked after to this day.

'I still think about him all the time and sometimes find myself wishing I'd kept him myself!' says Amy. 'He was such a brilliant little dog. Amanda and I agree that we'll never forget how it felt to save his life. It's a great privilege to be able to do that in our jobs.

'We're lucky we still see him at the centre sometimes. He's like any normal little dog now, bursting with life and love and happiness. He's grown a little bit but is still very, very tiny. His new owners bring him to puppy training classes and we can tell he remembers us. He bounds up to us, jumping up and down and wagging his whole body with excitement. Then he rolls over with his legs in the air to have his tummy tickled. Poor little thing, he sometimes get so overwhelmed with excitement when he sees us that he pees everywhere! I hope for his owners' sake he grows out of that habit, but they just ask who could be cross with a dog that happy?'

Tiny Tim was an unusually early Christmas reject for Dogs Trust to rescue. It's normally in February and March that a flurry of unwanted presents comes in to the rehoming centres. 'It's when the owners get bored of the responsibility or realise they don't have the time in their lives for a dog.' Amanda says. 'We do our very best to help and rehome those abandoned Christmas pooches, but there's only so much we can do. Because they are so adorable, puppies are more often given as gifts than older dogs and it's so sad to think many of these helpless little pups will be abandoned.'

And not all of those rejected are lucky enough to make it to rescue centres. If the dog warden hadn't spotted Tiny Tim so miraculously that snowy day in Leeds, there is no way he would have been alive today. So to help prevent awful tragedies at Christmas time, Dogs Trust urges every single dog lover out there to spread the vital message:

'A dog is for life, not just for Christmas.'

A golden retriever's coat has two layers – the beautiful golden fur you can see, and a hidden, second coat called an undercoat. This undercoat helps a retriever stay warm and dry while he's swimming or in cold weather.

Ninety-nine per cent of all dogs' genes are the same. Only one per cent of their genes determine their breed.

In the middle ages, rottweilers were used to hunt boar, which are wild pigs with tusks.

You may notice that dogs turn in circles before lying down to go to sleep. In the wild, this twisted long grass into a cosy bed.

The dog who played Toto in *The Wizard of Oz* was a female cairn terrier called Terry.

Poppy's Pointers

The Big Decision

It's no secret that everybody loves puppies. Just one quick glimpse of a young pup causes instant gushing, cooing and *aaaaah*ing.

Humans instinctively fall in love at first sight with the little furry creatures! But the sort of love a tiny puppy really needs is far more special and long-lasting. They need proper love and serious commitment that will continue for many years and provide them with everything they need to live a long, happy, healthy life. They need owners who will still love them when they get used to having them around, when they grow up into adult dogs, and when looking after them is maybe less than convenient.

If you lavish your pup with this proper kind of love, you are sure to receive so much more in return, in the form of fun, nuzzles and fiercely loyal companionship. Being a dog owner can be one of the most rewarding experiences a person can have, but it's important that anybody thinking of taking on a pup makes the decision very carefully indeed.

There's the time involved, for a start. A dog can live for fifteen years or more, so this is a very long-term relationship. And just like people, dogs are very social creatures. It's not fair for the whole family to go off to school or work all day and leave a dog alone in the house, so you must be sure somebody has the time to keep him company. There's the cost of food, toys, vaccinations, pet insurance and vet bills to think about too. And then there's lifestyle to consider. Will a dog be able to live comfortably in your home, with easy access to a garden or other outside space where he can stretch his legs and go to the toilet? Are you sure you are ready to take him for walks every single day?

As you can see, dog ownership is not just about laughter, licks, wags, woofs, fun and friendship. It is also a very serious business. And with thousands of dogs abandoned every year, it's worth spending the time to think very carefully about whether you can offer a pooch what he really needs: a happy, loving home for life.

Choosing Your Pup

It may sound obvious, but lots of people forget that puppies don't stay puppies for ever. They get so carried away with the cuteness of a tiny pup that they don't think about what sort of dog he will be when he grows up. But this is one of the most important things to consider. For example, if you live in a small house, a great dane won't be right for you. And if you're planning on taking your dog on long hikes through the countryside every weekend, make sure you don't end up with a tiny dog like a chihuahua!

So put some thought into what sort of dog would best suit you, your home and your family, and then do lots of research. Read through books, look at pictures on the internet and talk to other dog owners about their experiences. Think about whether you would like a male or a female dog, and be certain it is a new puppy you actually want. Adopting an adult dog can be just as satisfying, perhaps even more so, as rescue charities often find them more difficult to rehome than pups.

If you would definitely like a puppy, contact your local rescue centre and ask if there are any homeless pups in need of an owner. And if you have decided you want a pedigree, there are breed rescue charities you can contact too. There's a good list of breed rescue charities at www.dogpages.org.uk/breeds.

Dogs Trust loves crossbreeds and pedigrees alike, and has seventeen rehoming centres across the UK with thousands of dogs looking for new homes. If you adopt a puppy from Dogs Trust, the staff are there to offer help and advice for the rest of your dog's life if you need it.

But if you would still like to buy a puppy, you must remember:

- NEVER buy from a pet shop
- AVOID anywhere advertising more than three different breeds
- DO NOT buy a puppy if you have any doubts about the breeder or situation – even if you want to

rescue him. It will mean your money will be supporting bad breeding, which will create more unhappy puppies in the future.

When buying a puppy you should first ask a vet if they know of any good, dog-loving breeders. When you go to meet the breeder and see the pups, make sure you follow these top tips to make sure you take home a happy and healthy puppy:

1. It's very important you see the pup with his mum. He won't be ready to leave her until he's at least eight weeks old.
2. You must also see him with the rest of his litter, and the breeder should allow you to handle the pups.
3. Visit the breeder at least twice before going for the final collection, making sure you handle the puppies each time.
4. Look at where the puppies are living. It's much better if they are being raised in a home environment, with everyday sights, smells and

sounds, rather than in a kennel.

5. Check that the living area for the puppies is clean, and that your pup seems alert and healthy.

6. There should be no runny eyes or noses, and you should see no sores, bald patches or scabs on the pups' skin. Beware of other signs of illness too, such as coughing, and do not buy the puppy if you see these signs.

7. Find out if the pup has been wormed and vaccinated. Some breeders will vaccinate puppies at eight weeks, before their new owners take them away. All Dogs Trust pups are wormed and vaccinated before they are rehomed.

8. If possible, ask the breeder to sign an agreement saying you can take the puppy back if your vet looks at him within forty-eight hours and finds he is unhealthy. This would of course be heartbreaking, but again, it's much better to do this than give money to bad breeders.

Settling In

Once you have chosen your lovely new pup, it's important you plan how you will settle him into your home. It's always a bit stressful changing surroundings, even more so if you're a puppy and only a few weeks old! But there are things you can do to give your new furry family member the best start in life.

Firstly, decide on a name (Poppy's always a good choice, in my opinion) because this will be one of the first things your pup learns. He or she will start to feel more settled as soon as a doggy identity is established.

Then get all the necessary equipment. Your puppy will need:

- a feeding bowl
- a water bowl
- some newspaper
- a couple of safe toys

- suitable grooming equipment for the fur type
- a lead
- a collar
- a name tag
- a supply of food

You should ask the breeder or rehoming centre beforehand what sort of food he is used to and start with that.

Then you need to make a decision about where the puppy will sleep. Get a suitable bed and make it cosy with a blanket or an old jumper. Lots of young pups find it upsetting at first to be separated from their mum and littermates, and so are happier if they can sleep in their new owner's bedroom. Most dogs always like company when they sleep, but if this isn't practical in the long-term, you can move the bed somewhere else in the house once they have settled in properly.

Before bringing your pup home you must make sure your home is 'puppy-proofed'. That means putting away anything you don't want to be chewed, especially electrical wires because chewing through those could be very dangerous. You should also check to see that garden fences and gates are secure so you know your pup is safe.

Once everything is prepared, you are ready to go and collect your new four-legged friend. If he has come from a rehoming centre, make sure you listen carefully to any instructions given by the staff. If he has already been vaccinated, they should give you a certificate, plus details of any other medical treatment he may have received. And they should also give you leaflets about feeding, basic training and future healthcare.

If you've bought your puppy from a breeder, make absolutely sure you get all the proper paperwork when you go to collect him. This might include Kennel Club registration forms, pedigree certificate, dietary advice sheet and worming and vaccination details.

When collecting your puppy, it's best if two people

go so one can hold him on the drive home. He may never have been in a car before so it's likely to be scary for him. It's a good idea to take some newspaper with you too, in case he is travel sick.

As you are introducing your puppy to his new home, make sure you are kind and gentle with him, and that young children understand he is not a toy. He is bound to feel confused and strange at first, so you must allow him time to settle into his new surroundings. Show him where his bed and bowls are, and the areas where he is allowed in the house.

In time and with caring, considerate treatment, your pup will start to feel truly at home and your new lives together can begin!

Vaccinations

All puppies must be vaccinated to protect them from nasty doggy diseases. Every year lots of dogs are affected by illnesses such as parvovirus and rat-borne jaundice. If an unvaccinated dog comes into contact with one of these diseases, it could be fatal. Even the lucky dogs who recover could be left with long-term damage to their vital organs.

Vaccinations are therefore very, very important. Puppies can have their first vaccinations from six to nine weeks old, with a second injection at ten to twelve weeks. They will become fully protected two weeks after the second vaccination. After that, your pooch must have regular booster injections throughout his life to protect him from these horrible illnesses. Your vet can tell you how often he will need these.

Socialisation

If you want a happy, friendly dog that you can take anywhere and meet anyone, then socialisation is the key!

Socialisation is extremely important. It's getting your puppy used to people and other animals so that he isn't scared of them in the future. It also means teaching him that strange experiences, objects and situations are nothing to be scared of.

If a pup is not socialised properly from the time that you get him and throughout his first year, it can lead to serious fear and aggression problems in later life. Because Dogs Trust knows this, our puppies are always very well socialised. But if you plan to get a puppy from a breeder rather than a rehoming centre, do your best to ensure that the puppy has been bred and brought up in the breeder's home.

It's very important to start socialisation as early as possible, but it's also vital you make sure your pup is vaccinated first. This will protect him from diseases in other dogs and the environment that could harm him.

Socialisation is quite simple really! Let your puppy experience something new and praise good, calm behaviour. For example:

- Stand beside the road with your pup on his lead and watch the cars go by. If he sits with you calmly tell him he's a good boy and give him a treat.
- Ask a friendly person to speak to your pup and give him a gentle stroke under the chin. If your pup responds happily and doesn't nip the stranger's fingers or bark, praise him and ask the stranger to give him a treat.
- Let your puppy meet a friend's well-behaved adult dog in your garden on a regular basis. Watch them closely and see how your puppy learns his doggy social skills. Praise your pup for gentle play and friendliness towards the other dog. And remember, it's OK for the older dog to tell your puppy off if he bites too hard or forgets his manners!

You don't want to encourage fear in your puppy, so if he shows a nervous reaction to anything new, remove him from what's scaring him and try again later. Try not to expose him to too many new things at once, and if he has a really terrified reaction to anything, then ask your vet for advice.

Understanding Each Other

I could have called this section 'training' but I like to think of it as 'understanding each other'. Most puppies are eager to please and need only to understand what you want from them, but it's up to you to develop this understanding. And it's vital that any method of training that you use is based on kindness and fairness to your pooch.

First, get a book that can help you with basic training techniques. Dogs Trust have marvellous fact sheets too, called 'Basic Dog Training', 'Socialisation' and 'Housetraining'.

You should start teaching your puppy straight away so he doesn't develop bad habits. Teach him what is acceptable and show him what you would like him to do making clear, simple commands.

Your pup's lessons should be short and at regular intervals. And remember, because most puppies are anxious to do the right thing, it will always be most effective to reward 'good' behaviour and ignore 'bad' behaviour. Punishing your pup for doing something badly will only make him stressed and nervous.

A great way to reward good behaviour is through playing together, and of course this will also help you to build a happy relationship with your dog. As well as playing with people, it's a good idea to let your pup play with a grown-up dog too. If you don't have one at home, try to find someone you know with a calm, friendly dog and let them spend regular time together. All pups and dogs need to interact with others to stay happy and healthy, and to learn normal doggy behaviour.

To housetrain your puppy quickly, you'll need to take him outside every hour. Puppies have very weak bladder control and need to go to the loo very regularly throughout the day. There is a pattern to this: after they wake up, after exercise or play, and after each meal. So you should always take your pup to the same place in the garden at these times and stay with him until he has been to the toilet, then give him lots of praise. Remember he is only a baby and accidents will happen. If you catch your pup relieving himself in the house, just take him outside to the toilet spot and praise him. Never hit the puppy or shout, as this will just confuse him and probably make matters worse.

You should also ask your vet if they know of any good puppy socialisation and training classes. Make sure you visit the class first, so you know it will suit you and your pup. And remember a good class will get booked up quickly, so you might need to register in advance.

Training a pup can be very satisfying. Once you and your puppy start to have a better understanding of each other, you will both feel happy because you are creating a bond that can never be broken.

Exercise and Rest

New pups may look as if they have limitless energy, but you would be surprised to know that too much exercise can be bad for your puppy. Over-activity can lead to problems with bone growth, especially in some of the larger breeds. Your puppy will get all the exercise he needs running about in the house and garden for the first few weeks. However, you should avoid letting him climb the stairs or furniture, or doing any other tiring exercise that might cause him to get hurt.

Just like a new baby, your puppy will need lots of sleep when he is very young. You should encourage him to rest, and don't wake him up when he's sleeping.

It's also important that your pup learns to spend short periods of time on his own so that he doesn't develop separation anxiety as he gets older. If you have another dog or friendly cat, who will be home when you're not there, you should encourage them to bond as this will make it easier for your puppy to cope.

Feeding

At last we're covering my favourite thing: food!

Just like people, all dogs need to be fed on a balanced, nutritious diet to stay healthy and in peak condition. Your pooch can be fed on a 'complete' dry diet, tinned food and a biscuit mixer or home prepared food. The most important thing is that he gets all his vital nutrients.

You can buy all sorts of different types and brands of dog food from pet shops, supermarkets and online. Your dog's needs will change at different stages in his life, and lots of pet food manufacturers produce food especially for puppies.

They also make food for juniors, adults, old dogs, pregnant dogs, overweight dogs, and dogs with skin problems, behaviour problems or sensitive stomachs. Therefore you might change foods several times in your pooch's lifetime. When you need to do this, make sure it is a gradual process. Add more new food to the bowl and reduce the old food over at least five days to avoid upset tummies.

If your puppy has come from a rehoming centre, you will probably have been given a supply of complete dry puppy food. If you have bought him from a breeder, you will most likely have a diet sheet to follow. Whichever way you are feeding your pup, make sure you follow the food manufacturer's recommendations on the packet or the breeder's directions on the diet sheet.

Home prepared doggy diets are difficult and time-consuming, so if you can't put in the time, effort and expense, it would be better for both of you to stick to buying readymade dog food.

Most young puppies will need to be fed around four small meals a day at regular intervals, as their tiny stomachs cannot cope with anything bigger. As they get older you can reduce the number of meals per day.

It's important that your dog always has lots of clean, fresh drinking water, especially if you are using a complete dry diet.

And don't forget, treats are also food, so make sure you count them as part of your pooch's overall food intake for the day to stop him getting porky! As for what sorts of treats you should use: raw carrots, rawhide chews and safe chew toys are better than bones, which can actually damage teeth and cause problems in your dog's bowel. Also, lots of people don't know that chocolate made for humans can make dogs very sick and even be deadly, so make sure you stick to doggy chocs and other healthy canine treats.

Costs

When gazing into a puppy's eyes, it's unlikely that you are thinking about money. But if you are seriously considering becoming a dog owner, it should be one of the first things for you to think about.

Taking on a puppy means years of commitment, and much of that commitment is financial. There are things that you know you will have to pay for, like food and toys. These costs can vary depending on things like the size and breed of your dog, and you can work out if you can afford them by measuring them against how much money your family earns.

But those are not the only expenses to think about. A dog is a living being who, like a person, will have different medical needs throughout his life. You will be able to predict some of these needs – all dogs need vaccinations and routine treatment for fleas and worms, for example. But you cannot plan for your dog suddenly falling ill and needing emergency treatment at the vet's.

There is no National Health Service for dogs, and vet's bills can be very expensive indeed, so we at Dogs Trust always recommend taking out pet insurance. This means paying a set amount of money regularly to a company who will then pay for the cost of treatment if your dog gets sick. Visit our website (www.dogstrust.org.uk/az/i/insurance/) for a guide on how to choose the best insurance policy for your pup.

Pet insurance might seem expensive when you first think about it, but it really could mean the difference between life and death for your dog. It would be heartbreaking to have to have your beloved pooch put to sleep just because you couldn't afford to pay for his treatment. If he is lucky and lives a long and healthy life, you may never have to claim any money back, but at least you never have to worry about enormous vet bills that may be waiting just around the corner.

Neutering

We at Dogs Trust believe that every dog should be wanted and loved, but every year we see thousands of homeless and abandoned pooches in our rehoming centres. We think one of the best ways of solving this sad problem is by neutering. Neutering is an operation that means your dog will not be able to reproduce. Therefore no unwanted litters of puppies!

Unless you are planning to take the extremely serious step of becoming a breeder and know you can find happy homes for a whole litter of puppies, we believe all responsible owners should neuter their dogs.

As well as helping the homeless dog population, there are other benefits to neutering too:

- It can make male dogs calmer, less aggressive, less likely to 'mark' their territory, and less likely to try and escape to seek out a local female.
- It avoids the mess and inconvenience of female

dogs having 'seasons', and the strange behaviour that can happen at those times.

- It reduces the risk of both male and female dogs getting certain types of cancer.
- It reduces the chances of getting the large vet bills associated with certain illnesses and accidents caused by unruly behaviour.

Microchipping

What could be more upsetting than if your beloved four-legged friend went missing? Sadly, of the many thousands of dogs that get lost each year, less than half of them are reunited with their owners.

It is the law that all responsible owners must make sure their dog is wearing a collar and identification tag, but thousands of owners are now having their dogs microchipped too. Microchipping is the most effective and secure way of permanently identifying your pooch. A tiny electronic device is implanted under the dog's skin, between the shoulder blades, that has a unique number on it. That number is registered to the dog and owner, so when the chip is scanned, the owner can be found and the pair can be reunited!

The procedure doesn't hurt any more than a normal vaccination and costs twenty to thirty pounds. Or you can contact your local Dogs Trust rehoming centre, where we offer microchipping at a reduced price. We also microchip every dog that comes into our centres before we rehome them.

Your Responsibilities to Others

As a dog owner you must take responsibility for your dog's actions and behaviour. This is a very serious duty. Here are some of the things you must think about:

- By law you must keep your dog under control at all times and stop him from being a nuisance to others.
- You must keep your dog on a lead on any designated road.
- You are responsible for keeping public places clean by picking up your dog's poop. Make sure you always carry a poop-scoop or plastic bag to clean up after him. Don't worry – it's really not that bad and you will quickly get used to it!
- As a dog lover it is important to know that any abuse or ill-treatment of an animal is illegal. Please call the RSPCA's 24-hour national cruelty and advice line on 0300 1234 999 or the Scottish SPCA on 03000 999 999 if you are worried about a dog, or any other animal.

Poppy's Final Word: Your Life Together

I hope you've enjoyed spending time with me in this wonderful world of woofers. There is so much to learn about dogs and puppies that you could devote your whole life to it. Indeed, that's what our staff at Dogs Trust do as they work towards a happier future for our four-legged friends.

If you don't have your own dog yet, you can ask your local Dogs Trust rehoming centre about volunteering or fundraising with them. There's lots of ways you can get involved. Or to get quality doggy time in another way, why not ask a dog-owning friend or neighbour if you can go with them on their walks?

If you are lucky enough to be a dog owner yourself, the most important thing is to make sure you go through life hand-in-paw together. A lot can happen in your life during the fifteen or so years that you have your dog. There will be happy times, sad times, difficult and exciting times, and even times of big changes and new directions.

But one thing you must never forget during all these times is that the love and support of a dog is one of the most valuable things a person can have. They are happy to see you and sad when you leave, and always eager to take part in your fun. They delight in your happiness, comfort you in your sadness and feel all your emotions in between. And when the world seems complicated and confusing, they show you that the best medicine can be a lovely walk and simple game of fetch in the fresh air.

When you consider all that dogs give to people, they ask for so little in return. But what they do need, they need consistently and for their whole lives. That's why, when you see a puppy, one of the first things you should think (after wow!, ahhhhh! and perhaps eeeeeee!) is Dogs Trust's famous saying:

'A dog is for life, not just for Christmas.'

With all my love and lurcher licks

Your pal,

Poppy xxx

About Dogs Trust

Dogs Trust is the UK's largest dog welfare charity and we are working towards the day when all dogs can enjoy a happy life, free from the threat of unnecessary destruction.

We would like to solve the problem of so many unwanted dogs in the UK. We aim to do this by raising awareness about dogs, promoting dog welfare and encouraging responsible dog ownership.

We have seventeen rehoming centres across the UK and help over 16,000 stray and abandoned dogs every year to find new, happy homes. We never put a healthy dog to sleep.

How to Help

There are lots of ways you can support all our wonderful work for woofers in need. For example, many people like to help us through fundraising. Each year hundreds of people throughout the country take part in or organise events to raise money for our four-legged friends.

Find out more at

www.dogstrust.org.uk/howtohelp/fundraiseforus

You can also sponsor a dog by visiting

www.dogstrust.org.uk/sponsor_a_dog

If you would like to make a donation to Dogs Trust, you can do this at

www.dogstrust.org.uk/howtohelp/donations

Dog-loving shopaholics can buy all sorts of doggy delights and support Dogs Trust at the same time. Just visit www.dogstrust.org.uk/howtohelp/shopping

Contact Information

All the information you need about Dogs Trust can be found at www.dogstrust.org.uk, and there is also a special website for children and teachers at www.learnwithdogs.co.uk.

You can contact Dogs Trust's Head Office by writing to:

Dogs Trust
17 Wakley Street
London
EC1V 7RQ
Or telephone: 020 7837 0006

To find your local Dogs Trust rehoming centre, visit www.dogstrust.org.uk/rehoming/our_centres

Or if you already know where your local rehoming centre is and would like to help out, you can contact them on the telephone numbers listed on the following page.

Poppy's Puppies

Ballymena	028 2565 2977
Bridgend	01656 725219
Canterbury	01227 792505
Darlington	01325 333114
Evesham	01386 830613
Glasgow	0141 773 5130
Ilfracombe	01271 812709
Kenilworth	01926 484398
Leeds	0113 281 4920
London (Harefield)	0845 076 3647
Merseyside	0151 480 0660
Newbury	01488 658391
Roden	01952 770225
Salisbury	01980 629634
Shoreham	01273 452576
Snetterton	01953 498377
West Calder	01506 873459

Photo Credits

Meet **POPPY** the Dogs Trust office dog and read more heart-warming and unforgettable stories about some of the thousands of dogs rescued by the Dogs Trust.

Poppy was born in the Dogs Trust rehoming centre on Merseyside. The shoe-sized puppy was happily rehomed, but just two weeks later, Poppy became seriously ill and was rushed straight to the vet's. She was still so tiny that she might not survive ...

❧ Puppytalk ❧

50 ways to make friends with your puppy

Would you like to make friends with your puppy?
This little book shows you how with lots of interesting
and helpful tips that cover everything you need to know.

🐾 What your puppy is trying to tell you
🐾 Games your puppy will love
🐾 How to talk to your puppy
🐾 Ways to make your puppy happy

With the help of Puppytalk you'll soon be your
puppy's best friend!